AF411985

CONFUCIAN TRADITION AND GLOBAL EDUCATION

Confucian Tradition and Global Education

Wm. Theodore de Bary

with contributions by

Cheung Chan Fai and Kwan Tze-wan

The Tang Chun-I Lectures for 2005

The Chinese University Press
Hong Kong

COLUMBIA

Columbia University Press
New York

Columbia University Press wishes to express its appreciation for assistance given by the Chiang Ching-kuo Foundation for International Scholarly Exchange in the publication of this book.

Tang Chun-I Lecture Series

The Tang Chun-I Lecture Series is based on lectures and seminars delivered by distinguished scholars who are holding the Tang Chun-I Visiting Professorship at The Chinese University of Hong Kong. This professorship was initiated in 2003 by the Department of Philosophy, The Chinese University of Hong Kong, in memory of the late Professor Tang Chun-I (1909–1978), a major figure in twentieth-century Chinese philosophy and the first Chair Professor of the Department of Philosophy.

ISBN-10: The Chinese University Press 962–996–304–3
ISBN-13: The Chinese University Press 978–962–996–304–0

Published for North America and Europe by:
  Columbia University Press
  Publishers Since 1893
  New York   Chichester, West Sussex

Published for the rest of the world by:
  The Chinese University Press
  The Chinese University of Hong Kong
  Sha Tin, N.T., Hong Kong
  Fax: +852 2603 6692
       +852 2603 7355
  E-mail: cup@cuhk.edu.hk
  Web site: www.chineseupress.com

Library of Congress Cataloging-in-Publication Data
De Bary, William Theodore, 1919–
   Confucian tradition and global education/Wm. Theodore de Bary,
with contributions by Cheung Chan Fai and Kwan Tze-wan.
     p. cm.
"The Tang Chun-I lectures for 2005."
Includes bibliographical references and index.
ISBN 0-231-14120-3 (alk. paper)
1. International education. 2. Confucian education. 3. Tang, Junyi, 1909–1978. I. Title.

LC1090.D35 2007
370.116—dc22

Columbia University Press books are printed on permanent
and durable acid-free paper.
Printed in the United States of America
c 10 9 8 7 6 5 4 3 2 1

To Tang Junyi

He who would serve as a leader must be stouthearted and enduring, for his burden is heavy and his Way is long. To be truly humane is the burden he takes upon himself; is that not heavy? His Way lasts until death—is that not long?

—The Analects of Confucius 8:7

Contents

Preface   ix

Personal Prologue   1

1. Confucian Education and "The Point of Democracy" . . .   5

2. Asian Classics and Global Education   23

3. Translating the Classics   43

4. Tang Junyi and the Philosophy of "General
    Education"   59
    Cheung Chan Fai

5. The Overdominance of English in Global Education:
    A Glocal Response   75
    Kwan Tze-wan

Appendix 1. Life Chronology of Tang Junyi   101
    Lau Kwok-keung

Appendix 2. The Chinese at Columbia: A Personal
    Testament   105

Preface

The primary contents of this book are the lectures I was invited to give at The Chinese University of Hong Kong, in January 2005, in honor of Tang Junyi, a principal founder of New Asia College and a major figure in the preservation and development of Chinese philosophy in the post–World War II era. These lectures coincided with other recent developments in Hong Kong that related to my chosen theme of Confucian Humanism and Global Education; first, an address I was asked to give to Columbia alumni in Hong Kong and to the Asia Society of Hong Kong; and second, presentations made by two members of the Philosophy Department at the Chinese University, namely Professor Cheung Chan Fai's "Tang Junyi and the Philosophy of 'General Education'" and Professor Kwan Tze-wan's "The Overdominance of English in Global Education." Since their essays raise fundamental questions directly related to my own theme, I think they should be given a voice here as part of a symposium on the future of Chinese education in a global setting—a main issue addressed by Professor Tang himself. These essays are brought together here as our joint tribute to this esteemed scholar and teacher.

Professor Wm. Theodore de Bary.

From left to right: Professor Kwan Tze-wan, Professor Wm. Theodore de Bary, Professor Kenneth Young.

Front row from left: Mrs. Kwan, Professor Kwan Tze-wan, Professor Wm. Theodore de Bary, Mrs. de Bary, Professor Kenneth Young. Back row from left: Professor Cheung Chan Fai, Professor Chad Hansen, Professor Chris Fraser, Professor Lau Kwok-ying, Profesor Cheng Chung-Yi, Professor Liu Xiaogan, Professor Shih Yuan-kang, Professor Li Hon-lam, Professor Lau Kwok-keung, Rev. Professor Louis Ha, Dr. Leung Mei-yee.

CONFUCIAN TRADITION AND
GLOBAL EDUCATION

Personal Prologue

My first contacts with Tang Chun-I (Junyi), in the early days of what was to become known in 1949 as New Asia College, came as a result of my studies of Huang Zongxi (1610–1695) during the late 1940s. My initial interest in Huang was mainly in his political thought, in connection with his *Mingyi daifang lu* (translated and published by me as *Waiting for the Dawn*),[1] but as I pursued my interest in Huang's other major works I came to recognize the positive importance he attached to the development of Neo-Confucian philosophy, a subject that up to the 1940s in the West had become widely discounted as no more than a reactionary ideology supportive of repressive regimes both in China and in East Asia as a whole.

Yet this negative view was not confined to the West alone; it was shared as well by revolutionary movements in China, including the May Fourth movement, whose virulent hostility to Confucianism accounts for the fact that in the late 1940s scholars like Tang and his colleague at New Asia College, Qian Mu, felt it necessary to escape Communist control and try to carry on their work in Hong Kong. In this respect there is a strong similarity in their founding of New Asia College in Hong Kong to the founding of the New School in New York, where émigré scholars fleeing Nazi and Stalinist oppression in the 1930s and 1940s took refuge and founded a university in exile.

The greatest benefit that I gained from the work of Professor Tang came from his exposition of the Neo-Confucian philosophy of human nature and the moral mind-and-heart, which had also been a prime focus of Huang Zongxi's earlier accounts of Song and Ming philosophy. This led me to invite Tang to join in my Neo-Confucian seminar at Columbia, and to participate in two successive conferences devoted to Song and Ming thought that I conducted under the auspices of the American Council of Learned Societies.

Two articles of his were published in the proceedings of these conferences, the second volume of which, *The Unfolding of Neo-Confucianism,* was dedicated to him. In this way his work was shared with young American and European scholars, who went on to celebrate and develop it in their own way.

The other scholar at New Asia College to whose work I became indebted at this time was the aforementioned Qian Mu, whose accounts of the intellectual history of the Song, Ming, and Qing periods supplemented the more philosophical work of Tang Junyi in identifying the philosophy of human nature and the moral mind as the core of all Neo-Confucian thought. Qian, dealing with a broader range of Chinese thinkers in historical context, emphasized both the commonalities and the individual differences among them, and minimized the tendency to categorize them into separate schools of Principle or the Mind. I have discussed this matter in *The Message of the Mind in Neo-Confucianism,*[2] but when I was asked to give the Qian Mu lectures at New Asia College in 1982, I chose to speak on the topic "The Liberal Tradition in China," which would be inclusive of the work of both Tang and Qian as liberals in the broader sense of a social and cultural liberalism—that is, as the term would be understood in the expression "liberal education," "liberal arts," or "liberal learning." Both Tang and Qian would qualify as liberals in this mode, but in this lecture today I wish to invoke the larger tradition they spoke for and emphasize its relevance to the potential political uses of Confucianism in the contemporary world. Although New Asia College was not meant to advance a political ideology or agenda, I believe that the founding fathers of the college, in speaking of a "New Asia," implicitly addressed the problem of Confucianism as a philosophy that bore on the modern situation of Asia as a whole and not China alone. As indicated in their joint manifesto on "The Reconstruction of Chinese Culture" (initially drafted by Tang), the authors spoke of Confucianism among the shared values of "the East" as particularly relevant to the political, social, and economic challenges of the West. Thus, each in his own way—Tang speaking for the dynamic agency of the moral mind and Confucian spirituality while Qian spoke more for the scholarly mind and Confucian intellectuality—contributed something to what later became the "Asian Values" debate. For the invitation to honor Professor Tang on this occasion I wish to thank the Department of Philosophy of The

Chinese University of Hong Kong and especially the gracious hospitality of Professor and Mrs. Kwan Tze-wan.

Notes

1. Wm. Theodore de Bary, *Waiting for the Dawn* (New York: Columbia University Press, 1989).
2. Wm. Theodore de Bary, *The Message of the Mind in Neo-Confucianism* (New York: Columbia University Press, 1988).

1

Confucian Education and "The Point of Democracy"

In addressing the question of Confucianism's relevance to education today, I wish first to note the views expressed recently by a scholar active in the current debate on Asian values, Amartya Sen, who is widely regarded as a kind of East–West guru on the subject.

In a lecture delivered at the American Academy of Arts and Sciences entitled "What's the Point of Democracy," Sen worries that some people believe the "clash of civilizations" is upon us in Iraq and the Middle East, as the violence there confirms their suspicions that the Middle East is "unready for democracy."[1] He notes that "there remains practical skepticism about the effectiveness of democracy in poorer countries," but argues against the idea that authoritarian rule is the only way to economic development, as a necessary precondition of political democracy. He believes rather that, in Asia as a whole, democracy has not failed, nor is it incompatible with Asian cultures.

"The Point of Democracy," then is his answer to the notion that "democracy is a quintessentially Western value." Instead he believes that democracy's essence, "public reasoning," is common to most ancient civilizations, Asia included: "Public reasoning, in various forms, has had a long history across the world and these traditions in diverse cultures make it hard to see democracy as an essentially Western idea."[2]

As evidence for this claim Sen cites the holding of Buddhist councils for the debating of doctrine after the death of Gautama

Buddha; the same again under the Maurya ruler Ashoka in the third century B.C.E.; and later debates over religious issues sponsored by the Mogul ruler Akbar in the 1590s. In Japan, he cites the example of Prince Regent Shōtoku, in 604 C.E., whose "constitution of seventeen articles insisted (much in the spirit of the Magna Carta signed six centuries later in 1215) that: 'Decisions on important matters should not be made by one person alone. They should be discussed with many.'"[3]

Perhaps this much of Sen's case will suffice to illustrate the "point of democracy" that he believes Asian civilizations share with the West. And indeed one can find in most Asian civilizations some elements of public reasoning that survived as cultural resources to be drawn on for the democratization of modern societies, inasmuch as they lent themselves to the recognition and acceptance of corollary values in the West. In this light, key Western democratic values could be seen, not as foreign or inimical or "clashing," but as, to some degree, congenial with Asia's own cultural traditions.

To illustrate the point, when the Meiji emperor, whose Restoration and Renovation brought Japan into the modern world, issued his Charter Oath in 1868, his inclusion in it of a provision for "deliberative assemblies [to] be widely established and [for] all matters [to be] decided by public discussion"[4] no doubt resonated with the passage just cited by Professor Sen from Shōtoku's *Constitution.*

Since both Shōtoku and Meiji are clearly talking about "public matters," their statements are in the same order of discourse, and the political analogy between the two is not too far-fetched, even though we know that, during the intervening years, the processes of consultation at the Japanese imperial and shogunal courts were far from public in the modern sense—which leaves questions in one's mind as to how much practical continuity there was between the earlier and later versions of political consultation.

The issue becomes murkier, however, when we consider the other cases cited by Sen. Ashoka's councils were concerned with defining ethical and religious issues, how to keep them from intruding into the political sphere and disturbing the peace—in other words, how to prevent them from becoming public issues, which Ashoka was prepared to do by force if necessary.[5] Essentially the same could be said of Akbar's theological symposia, which kept religious issues politically tame and preserved the peace. Public reasoning yes, and still a value within the tradition, but not necessarily democratic.

When I gave the Qian Mu Lectures at New Asia College in 1982, I had similar problems in identifying "liberal" elements in Neo-Confucianism that might be considered cultural resources to be availed of in support of liberal democracy—things like (1) the morally responsible, socially involved, politically committed conception of the self or person; (2) the role of open discussion and reasoned discourse among scholars and in academies (*shuyuan*) seen as centers for educating people for both self-fulfillment and public service; (3) the role of community compacts on the local level as meeting grounds for the discussion of cooperative activities among villagers; (4) the role of scholars at court in lecturing the emperor on the classics as relevant to public policy, etc.

These are all activities that fit within the definition of public discourse Sen cites from the liberal philosopher John Rawls as "a public framework of thought" that "provides an account of agreement in judgment among reasonable agents." It involves a "political willingness of individuals to go beyond the limits of their specific self-interests [a key point for Neo-Confucians by the way] and exposure to open public discussions and debates."[6]

At the same time, however, some of the criteria Sen cites "for constructive and efficacious public reasoning" raise questions with regard to the Neo-Confucian case, just as they do with the modern—for example, the need to "make social demands to help fair discernment, including access to relevant information, and the opportunity to listen to varying points of view," both of which are still qualified in practice today (as witness the need for a Freedom of Information Act to be enacted recently in the United States) as they were in Song and Ming China by the given social, political, and economic circumstances.

When Professor Sen speaks of "public reasoning" as characterized by individuals' "willingness to go beyond the limits of their specific self-interests," he touches on a conception central to Confucianism. Its conception of the self recognizes not only external limits imposed on the pursuit of self-interest, or even on the pursuit of certain ideal values, but also the need for an inner, self-limiting process by which opposing or competing values are held in a balance.

Here "going beyond the limits of self-interest" actually means that the true pursuit of self-interest for the Confucian can be achieved only through reciprocity (*shu*) with others—or a balancing of self-interest with the legitimate needs of others in the family, the community, the state.

When Professor Sen speaks of "the Point of Democracy" he is talking about values that he considers central and crucial. He is not exploring the outer limits of possible freedom or the "infinite variety" of democracy but the heart, the crux of the matter. In Confucianism this would correspond to its concept of centrality or the Mean—"Holding to the Mean" as, for instance, between commonality and diversity, the recognition of individual merit versus the leveling claims for human equality, etc. Hence the need felt in Confucianism for understanding the inherent limits of human values, the need for a self-limiting, balancing act among goods or goals of equal, or almost equal, value. Thus from the opening chapter of the *Analects* we encounter discussion of the need for the individual to keep a balance among moral concerns, intellectual curiosity, and aesthetic pleasure. From this perspective "the point" of any Confucian public reasoning would be how one identifies the pivotal issues in this balancing act among competing claims on one's attention and action.

Beyond this individual self-limitation there would be, of course, limitations imposed by circumstances, the objective (intellective) recognition of which might constrain action on behalf of any moral or rational purpose. A prime example of this would be education, the value of which was a constant in all forms of Confucianism, early and late. The essential importance of education to democracy (not mentioned but implied by Sen in the sharing of access to information) is no less widely recognized. But while the need of all for learning, and the importance of access to education on all levels of society, was a recurrent theme of the Confucians, in practice they were unable to fulfill their ideal of universal schooling for a variety of reasons—limited resources and the competition for them; the preference of many in a preponderantly agrarian and rural society to value practical skills and labor over those less directly useful to economic production; etc. The Confucian balancing act in this case took the form of recognizing that education was in part a privilege of the leisured elite, the few who bore a responsibility, as a cultured minority, for the welfare and guidance of the disadvantaged majority—the many members of society handicapped by limited knowledge—which raises the question of noblesse oblige as a democratic value.

To these limits on the material realization of "democratic values" as Sen conceives them, there were limits imposed by contestation among competing power interests and by their ideologies. These took several forms: the competition in education between humanistic learning for self-development and the acquiring of skills (mostly literary) needed to qualify for office through the civil service examination system; the transmuting in the Ming and Qing periods of values proposed for the conduct of community life on a cooperative basis (the community compact) with a system that put much more emphasis on conformity to state direction and control, etc. The values of the community compact were widely disseminated in East Asia, but they were adapted to local conditions and took forms characteristic of particular national traditions. Thus the kind of "public reasoning" that Sen sees as almost universal in different forms of "open public discussion" was widely differentiated in China, Korea, and Japan as the precepts of the community compact were adapted to existing social and political structures—or to developing trends like the emerging Japanese nationalism and imperial ideology of the late Meiji period (1890–1911), when these seemingly homespun precepts of the compact became incorporated into the celebrated Imperial Rescript on Education in 1890. "Be filial to your parents, respectful of seniors, kind and helpful to neighbors, conscientious in the practice of one's occupation," etc., took on a different cast when made to serve as a moral launching pad for national loyalty and emperor worship—so much so that the Japanese Christian Uchimura Kanzō (1861–1930) conscientiously refused to comply with the required daily bow in school to the rescript and the emperor's portrait. The incongruity between this Confucian civility—a democratic value in Sen's terms—and an ultranationalistic ideology and ritual is only too apparent.

Elsewhere, at some length and in greater detail, I have discussed the practical difficulties that have beset seeming "liberal" or "democratic" values in China, most especially in *The Trouble with Confucianism* (1991) and *Asian Values and Human Rights* (1998). Nevertheless, it remains true that Confucianism survived the practical failures, or at least limited fulfillment, of these "points of democracy" and is now considered a force to be reckoned with not only by traditionalists but by liberals like Sen.

Although Sen does not himself deal with the historical contestation or conflicted character of the traditions he invokes for their "democratic" values, their survival in some recognizable form (even though subject to local and temporal modification) attests to their enduring significance as historical artifacts. And if "artifact" suggests too concrete and objective a reality for what most people accept at best as intangible realities, survival even in this form is significant for what it can mean for our understanding of "tradition" in "diverse cultures" as Sen speaks of them.

Let me recall an earlier episode in China's twentieth-century history that may illustrate the point. It is Mao Zedong's Great Proletarian Cultural Revolution. In the late 1960s and early 1970s Maoists thought that they would bury Confucianism for good in the dustbin of history while Red Guards rampaged around China destroying the last tangible vestiges of Confucian influence in temples and libraries. At that time, enjoying in the United States the same immunity from Red Guard attack as Tang Junyi and Qian Mu in New Asia College, Hong Kong, I wrote, in my preface to *The Unfolding of Neo-Confucianism*, the following:

> The Chinese have thought of the Way (or *Tao*) as a growing process and an expanding force. At the same time, following Mencius, they have felt that this Way could not be real or genuine for them unless somehow they could find it within themselves, as something not external or foreign to their own essential nature. The unfortunate aspect of their modern experience has been the frustrating of that healthy instinct, through a temporary loss of their own self-respect and a denial of their right to assimilate new experience by a process of reintegration with the old. To have seen all value as coming from the West or as extending only into the future, and not also as growing out of their own past, has hindered them in recent years from finding that Way or Tao within themselves. The consequences of that alienation and its violent backlash have only been too evident in the Cultural Revolution. We may be sure, however, that the process of growth is only hidden, not stopped, and that the new experience of the Chinese people will eventually be seen in significant part as a growth emerging from within and not simply as a revolution inspired from without.[7]

Recognizing that Confucianism is an evolving process and not a static reality (as if it could simply be represented by Sen's citing the early *Analects* or Shōtoku's *Constitution*), we can, by taking into account its later conflicted history, better assess the claims of those who profess to represent Confucianism today.

Here I shall mention just two recent examples: first, the semiofficial exponents of Confucianism in Beijing today, the Confucian Association, which promotes Confucianism as a rather polite scholarly movement compatible with the Communist Party's monopolization of politics and sterilizing of effective public advocacy that might challenge its authority. Except for these limitations, it is a benign, genial form of Confucianism that this movement sponsors, and that could qualify as a platform for "reasoned discourse" in the academic sense if not for "public discussion" in the full political sense. The Association was liberal enough to invite me to speak at a major international meeting in Beijing in 1989, and, secure in the knowledge that civility and politeness would prevail, allowed me to give a keynote speech on "The Confucian Tradition of Public Dissent."

No doubt a contemporary version (and my second example) more acceptable to the regime and the Association is the one offered by Lee Kuan Yew, former prime minister of Singapore (now "Senior Minister"), who, in the aftermath of a failed Stalinism and Maoism in the People's Republic, has become the favored model of a vibrant state-sponsored and controlled-market capitalism in China. Lee has long been the advocate of a conservative Confucianism that recognizes the value of its family ethic to social discipline and the virtue of "loyalty" understood in the conventional sense of personal support for the leader (rather than in the Mencian sense of dedication to principle and outspokenness in its behalf). Recently Lee reiterated his handy version of Confucianism in a way that few could take exception to. Allowing for adjustments to changes in modern life (like growing equality for women), he still insists that certain fundamental values must be maintained:

> The most important are the five human relationships (*wu lun*) that impose obligations and rights between sovereign and subjects, father and sons,[8] husband and wife, among brothers, and among friends.
> They do not hinder the chances needed for success in a globalized

world but may have to be modified as women become equal to men, and in governance as kings are replaced by ministers representing the people.

But fundamental values must be maintained: the emphasis on responsibility for the care and education of one's children, to teach them to be filial, to be loyal to family and friends, to be thrifty and modest, to study, work hard and become a scholar, to grow up to be a gentleman (*junzi*); they have sustained the continuity of Chinese civilization and saved it from the oblivion that has been the fate of other old civilizations.[9]

Lee has been equally aware of the powerful cultural influences from the modern West that tend to undermine traditional discipline, which in Singapore he sees as a key element in the social fabric and the efficiency of its labor force. According to Lee, much of this has to do with the different status of the individual in American and Oriental societies:

> One fundamental difference between American and Oriental culture is the individual's position in society. In America an individual's interest is primary. This makes American society more aggressively competitive, with a sharper edge and higher performance.... [By contrast] in Singapore the interests of society take precedence over the interests of individuals. Nevertheless, Singapore has to be competitive in the markets for jobs, goods, and services.[10]

Lee is confident, however, that Confucianism will rise to the contemporary challenge; it is not simply the vestigial remains of ancient culture but something the survival value of which is attested by history. Learning and education, always a high priority for Confucianism, can be adapted to the new need:

> Chinese culture will develop, evolve and adapt to successfully industrialize and globalize.... The economy is driven by new knowledge, new discoveries in science and technology, innovations that are taken to the market by entrepreneurs.
>
> So while the scholar is still the greatest factor in economic progress, he will be so only if he uses his brains not in studying the great books, classical texts and poetry, but in capturing and discovering new knowledge, applying himself to R&D, management and marketing, to banking and finance, and to the myriad new subjects that need to be mastered.
>
> Those with good minds to be scholars should also become inventors, venture capitalists, and entrepreneurs; they must bring new products to the market to enrich the lives of people everywhere.[11]

In acting on this advice, according to Lee, the problem "scholars" will have is not to be found in any cultural resistance in the past to the promoting of new knowledge and technology in itself. Lee is confident that the Chinese and the Confucians have met this challenge before, and history shows that at least as early as the Song, the Confucian teacher Hu Yuan (993–1059) established a school curriculum half of which was devoted to specialization in the new technologies of his time—of administrative law, military science, hydrology (water control), and mathematics—an example favorably cited by leading Neo-Confucians like the Cheng brothers and Zhu Xi[12] as applicable to the needs of Song society. Nor is there any need for Lee to preach this new gospel to the generation of "scholars" educated in twentieth- or twenty-first-century East Asia. Those heir to Confucian culture elsewhere in East Asia have already been heavily engaged in mastering new technologies for more than a century, and with even greater intensity in post–World War II East Asia. Whether in Taiwan, Hong Kong, or on the mainland today, students are already almost totally immersed in the hi-tech R&D or business management Lee now promotes above all else.

The real problem East Asian educators and students are likely to face is in following Lee's advice not to bother with "studying the great books, classical texts, and poetry." Serious scholars and teachers are already alarmed at the neglect of humanistic learning, and those familiar with Confucianism realize how totally at odds Lee is with the Confucian tradition in this respect.

When, in the eleventh century, Hu Yuan recognized the need for the Confucian scholar to acquire specialized competence in one or another of the current technologies, along with classical studies, he did so in the broader context of a Confucian Way seen as including three main components: Substance, Function, and Literate Discourse. Substance (*ti*) consisted of the constant moral values governing human relations found in the Confucian classics; Function (*yong*) represented the socially useful forms by which these moral values were given practical implementation in different times and places; Literate Discourse (*wen*, literally "writings") represented the civil (*wen*) discourse by which both values and their practice were given public expression in civilized life. And when the great twelfth-century philosopher Zhu Xi, after citing Hu Yuan's school as a model for all, put special emphasis on the serious reading of texts—a reading program widely followed in premodern East Asia—he did so in a way that could well be understood as serving the purposes of democracy in the sense Amartya Sen has defined it: study of the classics as an exercise in reasoned discourse. Indeed if one wished to look for a "standard Confucianism" as a reference point for issues raised by Sen and Lee, one could find nothing better than the classic educational pattern so developed.

Although one cannot attribute to it a global scope in the modern sense, Zhu's philosophy did absorb external cultural influences, especially from the profound challenges of Buddhism, and it brought education in East Asia as a whole to a new level. Indeed I would argue that the Neo-Confucian educational experience, which came to be shared in many ways with Mongols, Manchus, Koreans, Japanese, and Vietnamese (i.e., global for East Asia at that time), still has relevance today in important respects to the issues raised by Sen and Lee. Let me explain.

Zhu Xi engaged heavily in the retrieval of classical and neoclassical texts as central to a core curriculum. But this centering process also involved refocusing and simplifying—selectively focusing first on key texts like the Four Books, and postponing treatment of the more voluminous classic texts. The conservative instinct of the traditionalist to preserve as much as possible of the record of the past was subordinated to the need educationally to deal methodically with the process of learning, and pedagogically with the need of students for manageable segments and staged sequences. For its time this was Zhu's remedy for the kind of classicism Lee today would like to dismiss as pedantry or antiquarianism.

Zhu Xi's philosophy of education was one of intellectual and moral learning for the whole man or person, almost from the cradle (the Elementary Learning, *Xiao xue*) to the maturity of the Great Man (*daren*) as the truly Noble Person (*junzi*). Lee Kuan Yew, as quoted above, acknowledged the importance of this Confucian ideal as part of traditional culture worth preserving, but he has not recognized how inseparably related it is to an active engagement with the classics.

A proper understanding of this matter is also important to dealing with Lee's sharp juxtaposition of Western individualism versus the priority of society's claims on the individual (as Lee characterizes the Chinese tradition)—a false dichotomy and specious reductionism on both sides of the equation. Actually what both

Confucius and Zhu Xi sought was a balance between self and society, as both spoke of "learning for one's self"[13] in the context of family and community. In relation to the study of the classics this meant first reading the original texts for their direct meaning to oneself, and then discussing this with one's colleagues or consulting traditional commentaries. (The possibility of such a "direct, personal" reading may have its hermeneutic difficulties but has its own pedagogical justification while deferring such questions of interpretation to a later stage.)

As a curriculum Zhu Xi's program led from a central focus on texts that initially dealt with key value questions and expanded gradually to a much larger body of literary, historical, and philosophical material, as well as ritual and current affairs, so that its highly focused starting point (the Four Books)[14] represented a centering only and not a narrowing of the horizons of learning.

The second stage of learning through consultation with others (fellow students, scholars, commentators) marked another key feature of Neo-Confucian education, "learning by discussion" or "discursive learning" (*jiangxue*) that distinguished contentious learning and scholarship in Neo-Confucian academies across East Asia, and qualifies them as "democratic" (in Amartya Sen's terms, or "liberal" in mine).

From these historical developments, what lessons or experiences may be drawn upon that could relate to the prospects for democracy, whether in East Asia or the world at large? Following are a few suggestions:

1. Confucian education from the start was focused on the self-cultivation of those who would become leaders in society, and much of what is said in the *Analects, Mencius, Xunzi,* and in other classic texts would still be applicable to leadership in the modern world. (When Alan Greenspan said recently that the establishing of trust in leadership was the most essential thing in a market economy, he was reaffirming in his own way what Confucius had said about trust as the most fundamental requisite of a civil society.)

2. The usual complaint about this leadership ideal is that it was elitist, and historically one cannot deny that some Confucians relied on their superior scholarly qualifications to a degree that would identify them as a separate social and political class. A key issue here

is the one raised by Mencius to the effect that those who would be entrusted with the exercise of power over others should be educated, trained, and disciplined to serve that purpose, since power unguided by proper human values could easily become abusive. In this respect Mencius (as well as Xunzi) spoke for a leadership class distinguished—and to some extent set apart—by its pursuit of noble ideals, which equally emphasized noblesse oblige: self-sacrificial service to mankind. This was expressed in a passage in the *Analects* attributed to Zengzi: "He who would serve as a leader [*shi*] must be stouthearted and enduring, for his burden is heavy and his Way is long. To be truly humane is the burden he takes upon himself; is that not heavy? His Way lasts until death—is that not long?" (*Analects* 8:7) This was a favorite quotation of such a liberal democrat in the twentieth century as Dr. Hu Shih. Would it not still apply to leadership in any democracy?

3. Whether Confucians considered themselves an exclusive political class is open to question. The text of the classic *Zuozhuan* describes a political process in which everyone participates on every level of society,[15] and when the prime minister Li Si called on Qin Shihuangdi to suppress the Confucians, he argued that they had influence among the common people and thus promoted opposition to the state.[16]

4. The extent to which Confucians remained in touch with popular sentiments no doubt varied from age to age, and from level to level of society. One assumes that local leadership was exposed to popular opinion at some base level, but how much governance was a matter of upward, vertical communication, and how much state policy was influenced by such sentiments, is a matter of effective infrastructure, often lacking.

5. Prominent thinkers in the modern period, like Liang Qichao and Sun Yat-sen, have believed that citizenship or popular participation in governance was handicapped in traditional China because people's loyalties were mostly limited to family and village, having almost no active engagement with the state. This view would gain some confirmation from the fact that leading Neo-Confucian thinkers like Zhu Xi and Wang Yangming[17] (or Yi T'oegye and Yi Yulgok in Korea[18]) took a strong interest in local community organization (*xiang yue*), cmphasizing self-help and cooperation among villagers, but they had almost nothing to say about the need for structures and processes intermediate between village and state.

6. During the Song, Yuan, and Ming periods (eleventh to seventeenth centuries) what served something of a bridging function between local organizations and the state—or to put it another way, an amphibian function between the teeming sea of local populations and the comparatively sparse corps of officials administering them— were regional centers of learning and discussion, local academies (*shuyuan*) where philosophical discussion (*jiangxue*) and at times something like public discussion (*gonglun*) took place. The fact that this same phenomenon appeared among Neo-Confucians in Yi dynasty (*Chosŏn*) Korean academies (*sŏwŏn*), and in somewhat different circumstances in the *gakkō* (domain schools) and *shijuku* (private schools) of Tokugawa Japan, suggests that schools were the natural habitat for public discussion in Neo-Confucian cultures. (Tang Junyi himself recognized this when he chose to identify New Asia College in Chinese as Xinya shuyuan).

I believe the indigenous character and widespread prevalence of these educational centers as venues for the scholarly discussion of public issues helps to explain why a major reformist thinker of seventeenth-century China like Huang Zongxi, in proposing mechanisms for the curbing of autocratic power, naturally turned to schools to institutionalize this independent function—that is, designating the Imperial College and provincial schools as official centers of public discussion.[19]

But when Lee Kuan Yew, as above, says that "traditional values must be maintained," to whom is he preaching? No doubt some good souls who take him to heart in the bosom of their families, but apart from this what institution or agency in the larger world would be able to assert and sustain "traditional values" in the midst of the wholesale technological, social, and cultural changes that Lee's "individualistic," "aggressive," "competitive" economy brings with it?

Neither Lee nor Sen speak to the actual means by which "reasoned discourse" or traditional values in educational processes could influence or modify the tidal change of globalization.[20] One thing is certain however—there is no longer, anywhere in East Asia, a traditional educational system consciously addressing the issues or attempting to guide the process. Everywhere in East Asia the modernization process started with a revolutionary change to a Western-style education based on technical specialization. Nowhere I know of is Confucian teaching a part of a general requirement, or is there any significant movement to include the study of the Chinese classics as part of a core curriculum. Except for a few excerpts found in high school courses, the classics are studied only by majors in the field, as part of a specialized departmental program, not as part of everyone's general education. In other words, study of the classics has been reduced to a form of postmodernist technology, yet one still not competitive with other technologies economically more useful.

This widespread fact does not offer support to the idea that traditional values will contribute much to democratization, as Sen hopes, or to modernization as Lee would have it. But this is not a new problem for the modern world. In the late nineteenth, early twentieth centuries, a similar trend arose with the "modernization" of curricula in American colleges. When language requirements were modified and modern languages came to be substituted for Latin and Greek, the effect was similarly far-reaching—the classics, no longer read in the original languages as part of the required curriculum, also ceased to form the bases of a classical education for educated gentlemen in Europe and America.

The response to this at Columbia in the early twentieth century was to develop humanities courses, with the classics ("great books") read in translation, as part of the required core curriculum for all students. It is not surprising then that more recently educators in India and Taiwan, reacting to the loss of any classical learning in their "modernized" curricula, have recognized the similarity of their situation to the one that gave rise earlier to the Great Books programs or core curriculum movement in the United States. Curiously enough, however, there were similarities also between this new liberal education in America and the classical education of premodern East Asia, so the possibility exists that a new core curriculum global in scope could draw on traditional resources both East and West.

The resemblance of traditional East Asian education in the humanities, based on study and discussion of the classics, to the conduct of core curricula in the United States[21] suggests also that the issues raised by Sen and Lee have their counterparts in the effects of globalized technology on any humanistic education considered essential to reasoned, public discourse in a democracy. Lee's proposal to pursue hi-tech training at the expense of "studying the great books and classics" coincides with a question prominently raised (in 2004) by Andrew Solomon in the op-ed columns of the *New York Times*. He laments the dramatic decline in book reading in contemporary culture, and the atrophying of the mind—"The Closing of the American Book," as he headlines it. Reading books, he says, "requires effort, concentration, attention. In exchange, it offers the stimulus and the fruit of thought and feeling." On the other hand, he says:

> The electronic media ... tend to be torpid. Despite the existence of good television, fine writing on the Internet, and video games that test logic, the electronic media by and large invite inert reception. One selects channels, but then the information comes out preprocessed. Most people use television as a means of turning their minds off, not on. Many readers watch television without peril; but for those for whom television replaces reading, the consequences are far-reaching....
>
> The Nazis were right in believing that one of the most powerful weapons in a war of ideas is books. And for better or worse, the United States is now in such a war. Without books, we cannot succeed in our current struggle against absolutism and terrorism. The retreat from civic to virtual life is a retreat from engaged democracy, from the principles that we say we want to share with the rest of the world. You are what you read. If you read nothing, then your mind withers, and your ideals lose their vitality and sway.
>
> So the crisis in reading is a crisis in national politics.[22]

I do not wish to burden Lee Kuan Yew with responsibility for all the damage Solomon sees done by hi-tech culture to democratic politics, but one can certainly recognize that Lee's modernized Confucianism conflicts with some of the essential values of the traditional learning that Sen, like Solomon, considers an essential resource for global democracy.

Let me conclude then with my own summation of what is required for an education that would meet the challenge posed by Solomon, satisfy the multicultural criteria of Amartya Sen, and remediate Lee's simplistic reduction of Confucianism to the service of a global hi-tech economy.

First of all, what should be done educationally may be viewed from the perspective of first East Asia as a whole and then of the global view taken by Amartya Sen. Lee Kuan Yew sees things from the standpoints of both modern Singapore and traditional culture. But the latter, insofar as literate civilization (*wen*) in East Asia is concerned, is based on the Chinese classical tradition. And if this is so, then one's introduction to the shared "classical" tradition should involve the reading and active discussion of classics like those included in Zhu Xi's curriculum (i.e., as a select reading of the Confucian classics), but also of non-Confucian Chinese classics like Laozi, Zhuangzi, Han Feizi, followed by readings from the general histories and classical poets but supplemented by major Buddhist scriptures like the *Lotus, Vimalakirti,* and *Platform* sutras, and later major works in the Chinese tradition that Zhu Xi could not have known about (including Zhu himself, Wang Yangming, Huang Zongxi, and classic novels like the *Dream of the Red Chamber* [*Honglou meng*] and *Journey to the West* [*Xiyuji*]).

If we are thinking about East Asia as a whole, allowances would have to be made for classics of the Korean, Japanese, and Vietnamese traditions—a major and primary part of the curriculum for each of these peoples, but also to be included within the scope of East Asian curricula centered on China, and part of any Western curriculum that attempts to be global in scope.

In my second lecture on "Asian Classics and Global Education," I shall go into further details of the content and method by which the Chinese classics (and Asian also) can be restored to a place in a modern humanities curriculum that is adaptable to almost any local situation but also opens out to a global horizon.

My argument so far has tried to make four basic points:

1. That Confucian education properly understood and practiced could make a contribution to the democracy of the future.
2. That in the modern world Confucian education has to be seen in an East Asian context and cannot be viewed as simply a Chinese matter. Hong Kong, like Singapore and Taiwan, is part of an East and Southeast Asian community culturally speaking, and this has implications too for an East Asian political community.
3. Since East Asia itself is now part of the larger world community, and deeply enmeshed in the global economy and technology, Confucian education will have to be seen first as based in local tradition, next as connected to East Asia, and then adapted to the larger world.

4. Following this process, I believe justice could be done to both Amartya Sen's concern for Asian contributions to civil, democratic discourse ("public reasoning") and to important values of the Chinese tradition that Lee only partially recognizes and appreciates. It would show too that Asia (Tang Junyi's version of the "New Asia") has something to contribute to the conduct of Andrew Solomon's War of Ideas, when, as Solomon says, "Without books, we cannot succeed in our current struggle against absolutism and terrorism." If "we are what we read," and this active repossession of the classics is part of civilized discourse (à la Sen), then an inclusion of the Asian classics is not something that can be sloughed off (à la Lee Kuan Yew) but part of what "we" read together, meaning both Asians and Westerners engaged in this struggle.

Notes

1. Amartya Sen, "What's the Point of Democracy," *Bulletin of the American Academy of Arts and Sciences* 57, no. 3 (2004): 9–11.
2. Ibid., p. 10.
3. Ibid.
4. "The Charter Oath," in Wm. Theodore de Bary, Carol Gluck, and Arthur E. Tiedemann, eds., *Sources of Japanese Tradition*, vol. 2, *1600 to 2000*, 2nd ed. (New York: Columbia University Press, 2005), p. 671.
5. Wm. Theodore de Bary, *Nobility and Civility* (Cambridge, Mass.: Harvard University Press, 2004), pp. 20–24.
6. Sen, "What's the Point of Democracy," p. 9.
7. Wm. Theodore de Bary, ed., *The Unfolding of Neo-Confucianism* (New York: Columbia University Press, 1975), p. 32.
8. Actually Mencius held the parent–child relation as primary and ruler–minister as secondary (derivative). See *Mencius* 3A:4.
9. Lee Kuan Yew, "The Culture That Makes a Nation Competitive or Not," *Straits Times* (Singapore), April 22, 2004, p. 2.
10. Ibid.
11. Ibid., p. 3.
12. Wm. Theodore de Bary and Irene Bloom, eds., *Sources of Chinese Tradition*, 2nd ed. (New York: Columbia University Press, 1999), vol. 1, pp. 587–590; Zhu Xi, *Reflections on Things at Hand*, trans. Wing Tsit-chan (New York: Columbia University Press, 1967), pp. 262–263.
13. Wm. Theodore de Bary, *Learning for One's Self* (New York: Columbia University Press, 1991).

14. Zhu Xi, "Personal Proposals for Schools and Official Recruitment," in de Bary and Bloom, eds., *Sources of Chinese Tradition*, vol. 1, pp. 739–741.

15. "The *Zuozhuan*," in de Bary and Bloom, eds., *Sources of Chinese Tradition*, vol. 1, pp. 183–189.

16. Li Si, "Memorial on the Burning of Books," in de Bary and Bloom, eds., *Sources of Chinese Tradition*, vol. 1, pp. 209–210.

17. De Bary and Bloom, eds., *Sources of Chinese Tradition*, vol. 1, pp. 751–853.

18. "Community Compacts," in Yongho Ch'oe, Peter H. Lee, and Wm. Theodore de Bary, eds., *Sources of Korean Tradition*, vol. 2, *From the Sixteenth to the Twentieth Centuries* (New York: Columbia University Press, 2000), pp. 144–149.

19. Huang Zongxi, *Waiting for the Dawn: A Plan for the Prince*, in Wm. Theodore de Bary and Richard Lufrano, eds., *Sources of Chinese Tradition*, 2nd ed. (New York: Columbia University Press, 1999), vol. 2, pp. 14–17.

20. For a premodern example of how classical learning might be combined with technical studies in a "modernized" and "democratized" Confucian curriculum, see the educational program of a leading Japanese Neo-Confucian, Hirose Tansō (1782–1856), in the early nineteenth century: "Hirose Tansō's School System," in de Bary, Gluck, and Tiedemann, eds., *Sources of Japanese Tradition*, vol. 2, pp. 287–293.

21. As an example of this, "active reading and discussion" and "reasoned, public discourse" come together in my own colloquia for undergraduates, graduates, or postgraduate scholars and alumni alike, in the following manner: Everyone is asked to do the reading in the expectation that they will, at the start of class, give their own reactions to the text and the problems they have with it; in this way, the agenda for class discussion reflects the shared, expressed concerns of the students; all considerations of theory, context, subtext, etc., are brought in only as relevant to the issues so identified, with the instructor responsible for sorting it all out and offering (proposing) his own conclusion at the end. Starting from where the students themselves are is a little like the Zen master asking his student to start a visitation (interview) by "offering his own mind." The rest of what we do fits the original meaning of the koan (*gongan*) as a "public case" rather than as a personal conundrum or private joke.

22. Andrew Solomon, "The Closing of the American Book," *New York Times*, July 10, 2004, p. A17. Mark Edmundson makes essentially the same point in "The Risk of Reading," *New York Times Magazine*, August 1, 2004, pp. 11–12.

2

Asian Classics and Global Education

In my public lecture "Confucian Education and 'The Point of Democracy,'" I argued the need, contra Lee Kuan Yew, Senior Minister of Singapore, that for those in East Asia whose cultural traditions were significantly shaped by Confucianism, some degree of classical literacy—some familiarity with the landmark texts of their own "humanities"—was an essential accompaniment to the kind of electronic culture that so dominates education today. And, commenting on Amartya Sen's views with regard to Asian traditions as contributing to the public reasoning or discourse that he sees as "the Point of Democracy," I stressed that the "classics" of the more mature Asian traditions, and not just a few ancient texts, should be part of this literate, public discourse.

Today I wish to amplify these points in regard to certain specific issues in contemporary education. The common denominator among all of our educational situations is (1) the challenge to sustain any kind of humanistic learning at all in the face of the extreme competitive pressures of modern technologies; (2) the need of most educational systems to reengage with their own local traditions, from which they have been largely cut off; (3) the need but also the difficulty of sustaining this effort, beyond the initial stage, to encompass other traditions so as to achieve, over time, a global literacy as the standard of what every educated citizen of the world should know in order to engage in meaningful discourse with other peoples.

Theoretically of course there is no limit to what one might hope to learn, and so it becomes important to start with some basic guidelines that at least work in the right direction. This leads me to propose some of the criteria by which selective judgments might be made in the choice of classic texts and how they might be read in a way conducive to anyone's liberal education (as distinct from the technical mastery of the specialist).

One of the initial assumptions of the original Great Books or Humanities courses, as conceived by the founding fathers first at Columbia and then Chicago, was that the great books or classics were products of a "Great Conversation" among great minds over the ages, a continuing dialogue over what constituted the monuments of past learning or landmarks in a developing discourse. This conception faced no difficulty in moving from West to East, and it obviated any temptation to think of the East as "non-Western." No assumption has been made of the superiority of Western ways or the primacy of a European canon, but only of the presence in other major civilizations, and in other major traditions of great depth, complexity, and longevity, of comparable discourses on perennial human concerns and issues, which we should try to make our own to the extent that translation allows.

This assumption of parallel discourses had no difficulty gaining confirmation from the Asian works themselves, but there being no such thing as an "Asian tradition" (in the sense of pan-Asian), some judgment has had to be exercised in identifying the major traditions or civilizations to be focused on in a one-year course; in our case Islamic, Indian (including both Buddhist and Hindu traditions), Chinese, and Japanese (with the later addition of Korea). That judgment, however, was almost made for us, given our prior and most fundamental assumption concerning the nature of any tradition or canon: that it be self-defining and self-confirming. Thus it was not for us to find counterparts to Western classic models but only to recognize what Asians themselves had long since ratified as works commanding special respect, either through enduring appeal or irrepressible challenge.

Within each major tradition, this dialogue has taken place through a process of constant, repeated cross-referencing and back-referencing, internal to the tradition and largely independent of external involvement except to the extent that, from at least the seventeenth century onward, writers in the West, great and not so great, have confirmed for themselves what important writers in the Islamic, Indian, Chinese, and Japanese traditions have long held in esteem. Thus in the Islamic tradition al-Ghazali and Ibn Khaldun have based themselves on the Quran and commented on the great Sufis, while European writers, no less than Middle Eastern, from medieval times onward have recognized the stature of al-Ghazali and more recently Ibn Khaldun. Something similar is true of India, with the Upanishads and the *Ramayana* taking up the discourse from the earlier Vedas, the *Gita* from the Upanishads, and Shankara from both. And it is true too of China, with Mencius drawing on Confucius, Xunzi commenting on both Confucius and Mencius, the *Laozi* and *Zhuangzi* taking issue with the Confucians, and so on. Almost all of the great classics of the Asian traditions have established each other as major players in their own league, members (even if competitors) in their own discursive company.

It is of crucial importance, however, that enough of the original discourse be reproduced so that this internal dialogue can be recognized and meaningfully evaluated by the reader. For the reader (discussant) to recognize and judge the adequacy of one writer's representation of another requires some familiarity with the original work.

Since our program at Columbia includes parallel courses in Asian humanities and Asian civilizations, with a more historical, developmental, and social emphasis in the latter, as well as other courses in Asian music and art humanities, the overall program is less bibliocentric than the discussion thus far might lead one to believe. But it is in the discussion of the classic works that one can most easily observe the kind of internal give-and-take that should be incorporated in the larger discourse aimed at here.

So fundamental are the foregoing considerations to any kind of multicultural education that just to include one or two such works in a world civilization, world history, or world literature course is almost worse than nothing at all. It is tokenism, and even if such a course is equally and uniformly sparing in its representation of all cultural artifacts, it is only tokenism on a grander and more dangerous scale. If one's initial framework is a civilization or humanities course already established to deal with Western models, the addition of just one or two Islamic, Indian, or Chinese works will almost always be prejudicial, no matter how innocently intended, for in such a case the individual Asian work, bereft of its own context, will inevitably be read in a Western frame of reference by Western readers. Even if the instructor tries to compensate for this by lecturing about the breadth and variety of the culture in question, the information still comes to the student secondhand, so the latter must depend on the instructor's word instead of the original word of an Asian author.

No one can prescribe a fixed number or minimum of classic works to be included in any such multicultural program. Nevertheless, one could offer, as a rule of thumb, that five or six such works are the minimum necessary to establish the context of any particular discourse to which one might hope to gain access, assuming that the works are well chosen to complement one another and suggest not only the range of possibilities within a given tradition but also how it has grown and developed from within. For unless the cumulative nature of the discourse—its continuities, discontinuities, and mature syntheses—is adequately represented, the tendency of the reader is to see individual works as in themselves embodying some static essence of the culture, rather than landmarks along the way.

Today in a multicultural education that serves human commonality as well as cultural diversity, both content and method may vary in different educational situations, but a core program should make the repossession (both sympathetic and critical) of a given society's main cultural traditions the first priority, and then move on, in a second stage, to a similar treatment of other major world cultures. Further, to the extent that time and resources allow, it would provide for the consideration of still other cultures that, for a variety of historical and geographical reasons, have not so far played such a dominant role in world history. (In the East Asian context I would certainly point to Korea in this respect.)

At least two other general principles seem applicable to this educational pattern or approach. One is that it is best, if at all possible, for the process to extend to more than one culture other than one's own, so that there is always some point of triangulation and a multicultural perspective predominates over simplistic we/ they, self/other, East/West comparisons. Thus, the Columbia "Asian Humanities" course includes reading from several of the major Asian traditions, which allows for significant cross-cultural comparisons quite apart from those the student naturally makes between his own and any one other culture.

If the effect of this is to underscore diversity, the second principle would be that any such treatment, whether of one's own or other cultures, should give priority to identifying central concerns (such as "civility," "humanity," "the common good" or "commonality," "individual and group," etc.) as basic categories or core concepts, but a main reason for starting the process with source readings or original texts has been to proceed inductively—to ask, in the reading of these works, what are the primary questions being addressed in each, what are the defining concepts and values of the discourse, in what key terms have they expressed both their proximate and ultimate concerns? Such questions may well be left open-ended, but for the time being, at this stage of the learning process and for purposes of cross-cultural discussion, we should be looking for centers of gravity, points of convergence, common denominators.[1] Why? Because as a matter of educational coherence it is best to work out from some center, however tentatively constructed, to the outer reaches of human possibility. And for purposes of establishing the grounds for carrying on civil discourse, some working consensus, initially tradition based but increasingly multicultural, is needed.

The priorities and sequence just proposed would, it seems to me, be applicable to almost any cultural situation. If one recognizes that other peoples will set their own priorities, one would naturally expect each educational program to repossess its own classics first, and then move on to ingest others. Indeed one would concede this possibility to others as of right—that in China's schools for instance, Chinese civilization would have priority over European; in India, Indian civilization, and so forth. Starting from the premise that every person and people need their own self-respect, as well as a minimum of respect from others, it is essential for each to have a proper self-understanding—to come to terms with its own past. This is essential not only to its own cultural health but to healthy relations all around.

The key to success in such an endeavor is how well one identifies core human issues and how one selects the texts that can illuminate these issues from among the larger body of works recognized as perennial classics in the respective traditions. This requires constant reflection, reexamination, and dialogue among world traditions. But as each civilizational tradition participates in this multicultural discourse, we can hope gradually to expand the horizons of civil discourse and the scope of shared civilizational values, which will be key to the solution of our common global concerns about the environment, human rights, and world peace.

The last major review of the Core at Columbia was undertaken in 1988/1989. By that time the term "general education" had come into use, not as a product of indigenous developments at Columbia but in connection with the transplanting of the so-called Great Books programs to the University of Chicago by Columbians like Mortimer Adler and Richard McKeon in the 1930s and 1940s, and then its retransplantation to Harvard in the 1940s, where "general education" became the expression attached to the program set forth in the Harvard Red Book of 1945.

By the 1960s "general education" had gained sufficient currency in the media so that Daniel Bell, reviewing the program in 1966–1967, used it in the title of his book *The Reforming of General Education*. Previous to this it had been known simply as the Columbia College Program or as Contemporary Civilization and Humanities, but the commission appointed by Dean Robert Pollack in 1988/1989, which I chaired, reexamined the issue and decided that "Core Curriculum" was a more appropriate term than "general education," because the vagueness and indefiniteness of the word "general" was susceptible to diffusive, centrifugal tendencies that led not to an integrated, shared learning experience but to the kind of disintegration that had come to characterize the Harvard program of general education as loosened up by Dean Henry Rosovsky. We wished to emphasize that the Core at Columbia focused on the central concerns of human life and human civilization, in contrast to the Harvard emphasis on different departmental approaches to learning, which appealed to the diversities of an intellectual smorgasbord rather than pointing to the commonalities of human experience—a smorgasbord without a main course.

The most frequent criticisms of the more unified Columbia approach, on the other hand, are that it is authoritarian, that it arbitrarily privileges a fixed canon of texts, and that the texts are Eurocentric (they are mostly by "dead white boys," as the saying goes). I believe these criticisms arise from misconceptions concerning the original nature and continuing practice of Columbia's Core Curriculum.

If the Core is thought to be Eurocentric, this is because it has been self-critical from the start—the West reassessing where it stood in a larger world—facing large questions with respect to the adequacy of education and civil society to meet the challenges of a changing world and problems of unprecedented magnitude facing global civilization.

The first response to this challenge was the "War and Peace Issues" course at the end of World War I, which recognized that civilization itself needed to be rescued from the aftereffects of the war ostensibly fought to save democracy. "Peace Issues" quickly morphed into "Contemporary Civilization" (CC), with a recognition that contemporary problems were not amenable to the optimistic and simplistic assumptions of those who underestimated the depth and complexity of the problems facing the post–World War I world. A review of these assumptions in greater historical and philosophical depth was what CC undertook.

In the 1930s and 1940s those who had led in the establishment of CC and Humanities programs advocated a balancing of the Eurocentric tendency by adding parallel courses in the Asian Humanities and Civilizations as well as Asian art and music humanities. This was done in the late 1940s and 1950s, and the Asian courses so designed for the Core have continued to be given ever since. Thus the Core as an educational program has not been Eurocentric in principle. We have Asian courses designed for the Core, and students who take them have a learning experience similar to CC and Humanities.

Fortunately, in the case of Asian peoples who have become prominent minorities in the West—East Asians, South Asians, and Middle Easterners—we have had a base to work from. Their traditions are represented by classic texts, as well as classic works of art and music, that lend themselves to the same general education treatment as in CC and Humanities.

The most recent challenge to the Core Curriculum as centered on the great landmarks of human history and thought has come from those who believe that priority should be given to theory—especially to different epistemological and hermeneutic theories. But as the German scholar Karl-Heinz Pohl at Trier University has recently pointed out, most of the theories advanced in the recent culture wars are matters of fashion and zeitgeist, fluctuating *a la mode*.… Their universal application … must be questioned because they have all been creations of the modern Western mind.… Thus if one focuses on the most up-to-date Western themes, China and the other Asian countries will always lag behind, trying to catch up with the hot themes of yesterday, not of today; … what now appears to be "haute culture" ends up being "*haute couture*," a question of style fluctuating *à la mode*.[2]

Whatever you call the works themselves—classics, great books, major texts—these are works that have stood the test of time, as most theories have not. They have challenged generation after generation and have survived repeated contestation. They speak to each other in a continuing dialogue in which great minds and great writers recognize and speak to each other over the ages.

By their very durability and substantiality they have established themselves as hard artifacts of human history. Everyone who has "taught" them, so to speak, knows that it is the works themselves that teach us. They are bigger than anything we can say about them, and that is why teachers often say "the books teach themselves"—they are that great.

But the books cannot do this unless you have people ready to set up the programs and keep them going—that is, the collegial bodies that take responsibility for education, as academic organizations only sometimes do for a defined curriculum, aimed at educating the whole person.

Let me illustrate the point by citing a traditional ritual that is followed every year at Columbia's commencement—the administration of the Hippocratic oath to the new doctors of medicine. This takes place annually after most of the deans have introduced the graduating classes of their schools. The deans' congratulations of their students has increasingly become a raucous circus, as each dean tries to outdo the other in boisterous cheerleading that would be appropriate at a sporting event, but unfortunately at Columbia occurs only rarely at our athletic field. But after the dean's presentation of the Medical School graduates he administers to them the Hippocratic oath. Suddenly all the hoopla comes to an end. Instead of the deans' ballyhoo of their graduates and the students' noisy hijinks in response—the business graduates waving their dollar bills, the journalists their newspapers—everyone falls silent, while the dean of medicine asks the new doctors solemnly to swear that they will practice their profession only for the good of their patients, and will keep inviolate everything they learn that should be privy only to the patient.

Everyone understands that this is serious business, and if one stops to think about it at all, one realizes that any profession should be practiced with the kind of dedication and humane respect the Hippocratic oath implies—true even for the natural scientists who might seem to be the most focused on the physical or material aspects of existence.

Now if we proceed to even a second or third thought about the matter, it may occur to us that this ancient rite endures from the remote past in the same way as the classic texts one reads and ponders in a core curriculum. Like the Greek and Latin classics, the oath comes down from a "dead white boy." It could be dismissed just as easily by those who advance a specious multiculturalism to denigrate the so-called Western canon. The fact is, however, that no Asian tradition I know of would not assent to the same values as the Hippocratic oath.

The deconstructionists could find as much to question about the attribution to Hippocrates as some do about the attribution of the *Iliad* and *Odyssey* to Homer. The postmodernists could problematize and contextualize it—to use their favored jargon—problematize it into utter meaningless, but even the advocates of high-flown and overblown theory have to fall silent in the face of truths so plain and homespun that no one can fail to be directly, personally moved by the simple human truths the oath conveys. Suddenly all present remember what commencement is all about, that it renews the commitment to learning and public service at the founding of King's College. We are in the personal presence of enduring truths—it is not a question of hermeneutics or epistemological subtlety, but whether or not we personally are prepared to live by these truths and give them new meaning in our own time. From my own experience as a teacher at Columbia for fifty-five years, I can say that the *Analects* and *Mencius* speak to my students just as personally as does the oath of Hippocrates.

Bringing East and West Together in the Core

The final stage in bringing East and West together on issues of commonality and diversity has been the planning of workshops and colloquia for the stage beyond the introductory Humanities and Civilization courses, whether Western or Asian, at which the products of the several traditions could be brought together in colloquia on key issues bridging East and West.

The significance of this project is that it can provide a model for integrated undergraduate education that focuses on common human values and issues while also recognizing cultural differences. Without the articulation of such common values undergraduate education is exposed to political demands for courses based instead on diversity alone—on a multiculturalism defined only in terms of minority representation that, with little concern for intellectual commonalities or shared human and community values, threatens the balkanization of the curriculum and fosters a radical extremism that is divisive rather than proactive in the service of common goals. The consequence of not moving forward toward such common goals will be for young people to be increasingly attracted to simplistic and separatist fundamentalisms—ideologies that narrow the vision and offer a specious "identity" to those who lack perspective on themselves and their place in a larger world.

By now the Core Curriculum has long since reached the point where, in capstone courses of the senior level, it could help students to address the issues raised by the political scientist Ira Katznelson concerning the future of liberalism. An essay of his in *Daedalus* concludes:

> Both liberalism and the Enlightenment within which it nestles advance a philosophical anthropology of rational actors and rational action, insisting that human agents develop the capacity to deliberate, choose, and achieve sensible goals. In their effort to cultivate such rational citizens, liberal regimes in the past have all too often imposed various limits, drawing boundaries that stunt the capacities of individuals based on their religion, race, gender, literacy, criminality, or colonized status. But after centuries of struggle about the dimensions of freedom, enlightened political liberalism today acknowledges *no* legitimate barriers to reason, hence no legitimate ascriptive barriers to liberal inclusion and liberal citizenship.
>
> The result is a deep paradox. The global appeal of an enlightened liberalism cannot help but jeopardize the local attachments, the historical particularities—the human plurality—that constitute its most important rationale.
>
> Here, then, lies liberalism's most basic current conundrum: How to

broaden its endowments in order to protect and nourish heterogeneity while coping with its perils.[3]

Katznelson's challenge is to both liberal politics and liberal learning in general, but a liberal education that is global in scope must be considered the first priority in preparing to meet the needs of either. This was, in fact, anticipated by a founding father of the Columbia Humanities course, Mark Van Doren, when, at the beginning of World War II in his *Liberal Education,* he foresaw the need for such an education to include both East and West:

> Imagination always has work to do, whether in single minds or in the general will…. Without it, for instance, the West can come to no conclusions about the East which war and fate are rapidly making a necessary object of its knowledge. Statistics and surveys of the East will not produce what an image can produce: an image of difference, so that no gross offenses are committed against the human fact of strangeness, and an image of similarity, even of identity, so that nothing homely is forgotten.[4]

Van Doren's language, from an age somewhat more optimistic than ours, may be less fraught with the sense of peril in Katznelson's essay, but it is no less mindful of the challenge for us in trying to cope with the paradoxical "human fact of strangeness" (the heterogeneity Katznelson seeks to nourish), or in possibly forgetting what is "homely"—the difficulty of making ourselves at home with, or making room for, others' most intimate and strongly held beliefs (Katznelson's "local attachments"). Here, however, it is to fulfill this early vision of Van Doren's, as well as to prepare young people to deal with the contemporary issues raised by Katznelson, that we have proposed a multicultural sequence for Contemporary Civilization, bringing students' liberal education to maturity on the senior level.

Workshops on Nobility and Civility

To this end a series of workshops is being conducted at Columbia that aims at the incorporation of East–West materials in senior level colloquia or capstone courses, building on core courses (Core Curriculum and Humanities) introductory to Western and Asian civilizations. Its purpose is primarily educational, that is, the continuation of a learning process that broadens the horizons and perspectives an educated person brings to the understanding of problems, one's own and those of other societies. But this continuing process of liberal learning could well serve as an accompaniment on the upper college level to work on one's major, and give an added dimension to senior seminar projects.

Because we are working in the context of a well-defined, sequential core curriculum, these workshops face severe time constraints, both with regard to the limits imposed by course requirements on students and to the time faculty can devote to any new venture on top of the already heavy demands of a general education program. Thus the achievement of a broad, multicultural perspective (spanning several major traditions) requires great selectivity and intense focus on key texts that speak to the chosen theme. One risks being charged with superficiality either in ignoring some relevant texts or not going as deeply into the chosen ones as their inherent depth might call for. This, however, is not an unfamiliar dilemma in liberal education, the practice of which is always a delicate balancing act for generalists, and always exposed to the complaints of purists and specialists.

In the three-tiered staging of the current series of workshops and colloquia, however, we have recognized that one must deal with major traditions in stages—not as static, timeless entities to be represented by only a few classic texts but as civilizational traditions that have undergone historical development. The idea here is to track their trajectories in the course of some historical vicissitudes, and try to identify not timeless essences but perennial human concerns, marked by shared commonalities in the midst of cultural and historical differences.

As examples of these concerns or perennial issues one may consider the following:

1. Nobility and civility (leadership and citizenship)
2. Religion and the state
3. The self, individual, and person
4. Law and constitutionalism
5. The good life
Etc., etc.

If this exercise has started with the theme of Nobility and Civility, it has reversed the usual approach of looking in the East for something like the ideas, concepts, or issues that are discussed in the Western traditions—like Mortimer Adler's Hundred Great Ideas in the Hundred Great Books—and instead takes issues prominent in the Asian classics at the dawn of civilization, when earlier concepts of status nobility, the warrior (samurai) ethic, and class behavior were subject to the test of universalizing civilizational values, and then asks whether the Western classics have something to say on the same issues.

The details of our readings and interdisciplinary participation, for both our faculty workshops and the subsequent courses offered to college juniors and seniors (who would already have taken core courses in the traditions represented), are presented in the following addendum. We have already learned much from these experimental efforts about what it is practicable to do in such courses, and we have compiled the results in syllabi and workbooks that can be shared with others, from whose own experiments we shall be glad to learn.

Addendum

Syllabus for Workshops in "Nobility and Civility, East and West"

For the first faculty workshop (summer 2002) and the following student colloquium (spring 2003) the readings were taken from the following list of works representing the classical periods of the major world traditions.

Classical West
Iliad and *Odyssey*
Herodotus and Thucydides
Plato and Aristotle
Cicero and *Aeneid*
St. Augustine

Middle East and India
Al-Farabi
Nizam al-Mulk
Shah Nameh (Seyavash)
Dhammapada and *Buddhacarita*
Bhagavad Gita
Artha Sastra and *Kama Sutra*

China and Japan

Confucian *Analects*
Mencius and *Xunzi*
Laozi and *Hanfeizi*
Shōtoku's *Constitution*
Saichō and Kūkai

When it came time to adapt this reading list for the faculty workshop to the syllabus for a student colloquium on the junior–senior level, the students had already encountered many of these texts in the core courses prerequisite to the colloquium, and were prepared to discuss them more intensely in relation to our chosen theme. However, they asked that the earlier sequence from West to East be reversed so the colloquium would start with Chinese and Indian texts and then go on to the West and Middle East. This resulted in the following sequence, which has proved highly successful and has become standard for the first (classic) stage of this colloquium series.

Analects of Confucius
Laozi, Zhuangzi
Mencius
Xunzi
Hanfeizi
Dhammapada
Buddhacarita (*Life of the Buddha*)
Lotus Sutra
Ramayana
Bhagavad Gita
Shah Nameh (Sohrab and Rustum, Seyavash)
Homer   *Iliad* and *Odyssey*
Thucydides
Herodotus
Plato   *Republic*
Aristotle   *Ethics, Politics*
Cicero   *Dream of Scipio, De Amicitia*
Plutarch   *Lives of Cimon and Pericles*
Old Testament/Jeremiah
St. Augustine   *City of God*

The Life of Muhammad
Al-Farabi

For the second workshop, the readings were taken from among

Europe
Dante Alighieri
Chrétien de Troyes
Geoffrey Chaucer
Thomas More
Castiglione
Montaigne
Molière
Thomas Hobbes

Middle East and India
Al-Ghazali
Maimonides
Usama ibn Munqidh
Ibn Tufayl
Averroës
Ibn Khaldun
Santideva
Visakhadatta
Ilanko Atikal
Manjhan
Sukraniti

East Asia
Lotus Sutra
Golden Light Sutra
Huiyuan   "A Monk Does Not Bow Down
                                            Before a King"

Sutra of the Humane King
Kenkō   *Essays in Idleness*
Tale of the Heike (for medieval Japan)
Zhu Xi
Wang Yangming
Huang Zongxi (for China)

Yi T'oegye and Yi Yulgok (for Korea)
Kaibara Ekken
Yamaga Sokō and Muro Kyūsō (for seventeenth- and eighteenth-
century Japan)

A third-stage workshop with the subtitle "Leadership and Citizenship" and dealing with the modern period 1800 to 1930 was held in summer 2004. It was chaired by Pierre Force (chair of the French Department) and Andrew Nathan (chair of Political Science) and included the following readings:

Western Texts

John Locke (1632–1704)	*A Letter Concerning Toleration*
Bernard Mandeville (1670–1733)	*The Fable of the Bees*
C.-L. Montesquieu (1689–1755)	*The Spirit of Laws* (first twelve books)
J.-J. Rousseau (1712–1788)	*The Origins of Inequality* (Second Discourse), *Émile*
Adam Smith (1723–1790)	*The Theory of Moral Sentiments*
Heinrich von Kleist (1777–1811)	*Michael Kohlhaas*
G. W. F. Hegel (1770–1831)	*The Phenomenology of Spirit* (on the master/slave dialectic)
Immanuel Kant (1724–1804)	*Political Writings*
R. W. Emerson (1803–1883)	*The American Scholar* / Self-Reliance (1840) / Experience (1844)
Alexis de Toqueville (1805–1859)	*Democracy in America*
Walt Whitman (1819–1892)	"Democratic Vistas"
Fyodor Dostoevsky (1821–1881)	"A Gentle Creature"
Leo Tolstoy (1818–1910)	"The Death of Ivan Il'ich"
Friedrich Nietzsche (1844–1900)	*The Genealogy of Morals*
Søren Kierkegaard (1813–1850)	*Either/Or*
Émile Durkheim (1858–1917)	*The Division of Labor*
Max Weber (1864–1920)	"The Profession and Vocation of Politics"

Middle Eastern Texts

Ziya Gökalp (1876–1924)	*The Principles of Turkism*
Sadegh Hedayat (1903–1951)	*The Blind Owl*

Naguib Mahfouz (1912–2006)   *The Thief and the Dogs*
Jalal Al-e-Ahmad (1922–1969)   *Plagued by the West*

Indian Texts
Rabindranath Tagore (1861–1941)   *Sacrifice, An Eastern University*
Mohandas Gandhi (1869–1948)   *Autobiography, Non-violent*
                                    Struggle
Aurobindo Ghose (1872–1950)   *Hinduism and Nationalism*
Muhammad Iqbal (1873–1938)   *Islam and Human Dignity*
                                    The Reconstruction of Religious
                                    Thought in Islam

Japanese Texts: *Sources of Japanese Tradition*, Vol. 2
Aizawa Seishisai (1782–1863)   *The National Substance of Polity*
Sakuma Shōzan (1811–1864)   *Eastern Ethics and Western*
                                    Science
Yokoi Shōnan (1809–1869)   *Opening the Country to the*
                                    Common Good
Fukuzawa Yukichi (1834–1901)   *Encouragement of Learning*

The Imperial Rescript on Education of 1890 and Commentary of
Tokutomi Iichirō

Yoshino Sakuzō (1878–1933)   *Constitutionalism*

Chinese Texts: *Sources of Chinese Tradition*, Vol. 2
Zhang Zhidong (1837–1901)   *Exhortation to Learn*
Kang Youwei (1858–1927)   *Confucius as a Reformer*
                                    The Grand Commonality
Liang Qichao (1873–1929)   *Renewing the People*
Sun Yat-sen (1866–1925)   *The Principle of Democracy*
Liang Shuming (1893–1988)   *Reconstructing the Community*
                                    (*SCT* 2:379–385)
Mao Zedong (1893–1976)   *Report on the Hunan Peasant*
                                    Movement (*SCT* 2:406–410)
Liu Shaoqi (1898–1969)   *How to Be a Good Communist*
                                    (*SCT* 2:427–431)

A fourth workshop on the same theme held in May and June 2005
dealt with the contemporary period (1930–2000):

Western

Martha Nussbaum (b. 1947)	*Cultivating Humanity: A Classical Defense of Reform in Liberal Education* (1997)
Norbert Elias (1897–1990)	*The Civilizing Process*
Vladimir Nabokov (1899–1977)	*Speak Memory*
José Ortega y Gasset (1883–1955)	*Revolt of the Masses*
Milovan Djilas (1911–1995)	*The New Class*
Hannah Arendt (1906–1975)	*The Human Condition*
James Joyce (1882–1941)	*The Dead*
John Rawls (1921–2002)	*Political Liberalism*
Charles Taylor (b. 1931)	*Ethics of Authenticity*
Isaiah Berlin (1909–1997)	"Pursuit of the Ideal" "The Role of the Intelligentsia"
Lionel Trilling (1905–1975)	*Sincerity and Authenticity* "The Heroic, the Beautiful, the Authentic"
Virginia Woolf (1882–1941)	"Mr. Bennett and Mrs. Brown"
Arthur Miller (1915–2005)	*Death of a Salesman*
Thomas Mann (1875–1955)	*Mario and the Magician*
Varlam Shalamov (1907–1982)	*Kolyma Tales*
Anna Akhmatova (1889–1966)	"Requiem"
Adam Michnik (b. 1946)	"Maggots and Angels"

Middle East

Naguib Mafouz (1912–2006)	*Autumn Quail*
Forugh Farrokhzad (b. 1935)	Selected poetry
Baqir al-Sadr (1934?–1980)	*Islam and Schools of Economics*
Larbi Sadiki	*The Search for Arab Democracy*
Abdolkarim Soroush (b. 1945)	*Reason, Freedom, and Democracy in Islam*
Girish Karnad (b. 1938)	*Tughlaq*

India

R. K. Narayan (1906–2001)	*The Guide*
B. R. Ambedkar (1892–1956)	*Critique of Gandhism*
Amartya Sen (b. 1933)	*Democracy as a Universal Value*

Japan

Ōe Kenzaburō (b. 1935) — "Japan, the Ambiguous, and Myself" (Nobel Prize Lecture)

Mishima Yukio (1925–1970) — "Japan's Imperial Elegance"

Ueno Chizuko (b. 1948) — "Problems of Japanese Feminism"

Maruyama Masao (1914–1996) — "The Basso Ostinato of Japanese Political Life"

China

Tang Junyi (1909–1978) — "Manifesto for … the Reconstruction of Chinese Culture"

Fang Lizhi (b. 1936) — "The Social Responsibility of Today's Intellectuals"

Li Xiaojiang (b. 1951) — "Awakening of Women's Consciousness"

Wei Jingsheng (b. 1950) — "The Fifth Modernization"

Gu Mu (b. 1914) — *Confucianism as the Essence of Chinese Tradition*

Notes

1. See the topics for discussion suggested for each major work included in the *Guide to the Asian Classics*, 3rd ed. (New York: Columbia University Press, 1989).

2. Karl-Heinz Pohl, "Reflections on Avant-Garde Theory in Chinese–Western Cross-Cultural Context," *Newsletter for the Study of East Asian Civilization*, no. 3 (April 2004): 2–3.

3. Ira Katznelson, "Evil and Politics," *Daedalus* 13, no. 1 (2002): 9–10.

4. Mark Van Doren, *Liberal Education* (New York: Holt, 1943), p. 127, quoted in Wm. Theodore de Bary and Irene Bloom, eds., *Approaches to the Asian Classics* (New York: Columbia University Press, 1990), p. 20.

3

Translating the Classics

In discussing the priorities that must necessarily be set between a global curriculum and local culture, I affirmed above that a core curriculum should make the repossession of a given society's main cultural traditions the first priority and then move on to a similar treatment of other major world traditions. At that point, however, I dodged a crucial question that besets any effort at humanistic learning that attempts to repossess classic works through an encounter with written texts, an encounter that is both personal and collegial. In what language is this to be done?

Obviously I assumed the answer to be in translation and not, for the most part, a reading in the original language. But the question raised by Professor Kwan Tze-wan in an essay reproduced herein bears significantly on the problem of how general education can be conducted today in a manner that respects the integral connection between language and the cultural artifacts that stand as commanding monuments of tradition. He recognizes, as must almost anyone engaged in education in the world today, that English has become the lingua franca of contemporary culture and of the economic and technical expertise that dominates the educational scene.

This practical dominance of English has become so pervasive, and native languages often so recessive, that in schools boasting of their advanced standing in preparing young people for success in today's globalized economy, English has tended to become the first, not the second language, for anyone operating on a high cultural level. As a consequence Professor Kwan agonizes over the threatened marginalization or even demise of the languages that historically have sustained major civilizations. Literate discourse has always been key to the civil discourse that constitutes the very fabric of civility and civilized life. May not what Professor Kwan calls the overdominance of English as a modern lingua franca undermine this civil discourse and hence civility itself?

Acting on the principle "think globally, act locally," Professor Kwan's answer to this question is that globalization must be accompanied by a serious and sustained effort at "glocalization," his homemade neologism for the conservation of local tradition by a conscious effort to preserve native languages in higher education. That this is not merely an abstract or speculative question is testified to by the proposal of some educators in Hong Kong to internationalize by letting English become the primary language of instruction—a policy that could hardly be more in contradiction to the original founding intention of New Asia College (the base on which The Chinese University of Hong Kong was built) as a university in exile meant to preserve Chinese culture during the Maoist cultural revolutionary onslaught against it on the mainland of China in the 1950s.

While Professor Kwan makes his own cogent case for glocalization in larger educational and philosophical terms, what interests us here more particularly is the relevance of the issue to the repossession of the classics as part of a humanistic education and core curriculum that can sustain a global civilization (and not just a global economy). Here we focus on the question of translation—first of all, the question of whether classic texts are translatable at all, in terms that do justice to the original, and second whether the reading of classics in translation necessarily jeopardizes the perpetuation of local traditions, or whether it may not be a means, a bridge between tradition and modernity.

Actually these are not new questions but are as old as civilization itself. English as what Professor Kwan calls the lingua franca of contemporary civilization was preceded by Latin and Greek as the lingua francas of classical Western civilization, just as Chinese was the lingua franca of much of East Asian classical civilization. The classical education provided by elite schools to young British and American students in the nineteenth and early twentieth centuries was based on language requirements in Latin and Greek, and many of the classics were read in the original.

The relevant change in the early twentieth century United States was the dropping of classical languages—Greek and Latin—from the college requirements, and the need then felt to preserve the reading of the classics, long thought to be essential for educated "gentlemen," in translation. When this change occurred, defenders of the classical languages argued against it on the ground that, if the classics were not read in the original, something would inevitably be lost in translation. That there would indeed be some loss in respect to certain values inherent in the original languages and literary forms could hardly be doubted, but John Erskine, the early proponent of reading the classics in translation, discounted that loss. "How many people read the Bible in the original?" he asked, implying that the most important values in any such works could still be appreciated, as the Bible was, in translation.

Indeed Mark Van Doren, who subsequently became a leading exponent of the Humanities, or "Great Books," program at Columbia, Chicago, and St. Johns, insisted that one test of a real classic was that it could survive translation even if some nuances were lost. He meant of course that such a work dealt importantly with issues, concerns, and values so pertinent to, and so perennial in, human life that any work addressing them in a challenging way would not become obsolete. If this is obviously so of the place of Latin and Greek classics in the English, French, or German heritages, it is no less true of the quick ascent and commanding position established by Shakespeare in European literatures and cultural idioms other than the English.

Nor is this true only of the West. Confirmation of it has come likewise from Asia—from classics of the several Asian traditions that have survived translation from one language to another—Chinese classics translated (adapted) into Korean and Japanese that have become no less accepted as classics in their adoptive land as were the Greek and Latin works in the classic traditions of Western Europe.[1] The same of course has been true of Indian works translated into the languages of South and East Asia, and now of Western works esteemed as classics in modern Asia.

Thus, even granted that something is inevitably lost in translation, it need not be seen as an irreparable loss. Translation of classic texts into the contemporary lingua franca may actually extend their bookshelf life in ways that have contributed and may still contribute to new civilizations (and thereby qualify or limit the "overdominance" of the new idiom). Yet this may also remind us that there is more to retrieve and repossess in the originals as part of an expanded classical inheritance. The efforts of pioneer translators (Western or Asian) to render Asian classics into Western languages not only enriched the cultural life of the nineteenth- and twentieth-century West, and especially the work of leading Western thinkers and writers (too numerous to mention) who recognized the value of Asian classics. They also had a kind of reverse benefit for young Asians who, initially drawn to the dominant modern Western culture and often abruptly removed from the orbit of their own classical literatures, were led back to their own traditions by the importance Europeans found in them as outposts on their expanding intellectual and spiritual horizons. Tolstoy is a prime example of the latter and Mahatma Gandhi is one of his beneficiaries, having, in the process of trying to convert himself into a perfect English gentleman, found his way back to his own roots with the help of Tolstoy, Ruskin, and the English Theosophists. Although Gandhi had no doubt imbibed much of Indian religiosity through his mother's milk and his father's strict example, he acknowledged that he had not learned Sanskrit and had not read the prime Hindu scripture, the *Bhagavad Gita*, until English friends impressed him with their own appreciation of it.

Gandhi's case is illustrative of another factor in the modern cultural situation that bears upon Kwan's glocalization. Early in life the influence of Indian tradition on Gandhi took the form of local custom and vernacular literature, not the classical Sanskrit forms, and it is significant that he had access to the more refined and culturally sophisticated levels of "his own tradition" as mediated through Western thought and scholarship. This could happen because the classical culture of India was more the property of an elite class, the Brahmans, than it was of the less privileged castes. Parallel to this we have the case of the elite of Boston society and high culture becoming known as Boston brahmins in part because their characteristic "transcendentalism" was much informed by Indian spiritualities identified with the Brahmanical tradition. Just as Gandhi contributed to the formation of a new, more democratic Indian culture through the fusion of Western and Indian elements, the Boston brahmins were doing something of the same for "New" England.

Although the Confucian Mandarinate in late imperial China was much less of a hereditary aristocracy than the Brahmans in India, still as the elite bearers of a high culture they faced many of the same problems in transmitting the classical tradition to twentieth-century China as did the Brahmans in India. Confucians lost not only their privileged position in the civil service, but even their identity as a distinct scholarly class, to a new educated class who often saw the classical language as an obstacle to modernization and advocated a populist vernacular as the only suitable medium for constructing a modern culture. This meant that the new generation of students in twentieth-century China would not only be following a modern, largely Western curriculum, but they would increasingly be cut off from the language of the classics, and forced to approach them through translations into the vernacular. Survival of the classics became a more and more tenuous matter; a household custom in elite homes for parents, concerned over the neglect of the classics in public schools, who resorted to homeschooling in a rather homespun attempt to remedy this deficiency. Apart from this it was only a relative few college students who read the classics as majors in classics departments. This does not mean that all traditional values were lost—some were preserved in proverbial form as part of family and village life—but while tradition can survive on this level as an identifiable element of folk culture, it leaves a large question as to whether this can be effective—that is, articulated—on the level of political and economic life that has to deal with more complex, often technical matters. Certainly it was on this level of civilized life and national decision making that the founders of New Asia College in the 1950s were concerned to sustain traditional values as still expressible in terms relevant to the formulation of political, social, and educational policy.

Although the founders of New Asia College sought to address this challenge in times of great crisis, as spokesmen for a Confucian diaspora experiencing unprecedented dislocation and extreme duress, their response to this extremity was not wholly unique but bore a basic resemblance to like efforts of Confucians in responding somewhat earlier to the challenge of modernity. A case in point is found in the modernizing reforms of Meiji Japan, through which a virtual revolution took place in the educational system. A prominent representative of the court nobility, Prince Saionji Kinmochi (1849–1940), assisted in the 1868 Restoration and was involved in many of the constitutional changes and new infrastructure of a civil society. Known generally as a progressive and a sponsor of Westernization projects, Saionji was at the same time concerned about the eclipse of traditional values and especially the loss of Confucian teachings, for which there was no place in the Westernized structures and curricula of the new public schools and state universities. Thus he lent his considerable prestige to the founding of an academy, the Ritsumeikan, which was conceived on the model of similar Neo-Confucian academies in the Tokugawa period. It was to be a counterpart to the new university, balancing, one might say, Saionji's part in the creation of the Western-style Meiji University while preserving the name and form of the traditional institutions (*kan*) most associated with Tokugawa Neo-Confucianism.

The other part of the name, *ritsumei*, is no less indicative of what Saionji and his collaborators considered the essence of both Confucian and Neo-Confucian learning—that is, self-cultivation. Saionji felt this was noticeably lacking in the kind of specialized, departmentalized structures of Western-style universities. The expression *ritsumei* was drawn from the text of Mencius, one of the Four Books canonized by Zhu Xi, and familiar to all of Saionji's generation (including the Emperor Meiji himself) as an integral part of their early schooling. *Ritsu* has the most literal meaning of "to stand, stand up, set up, or establish"; *mei*, literally "command" or "charge," has connotations also of what Heaven ordains as one's fate, destiny, or mission in life. For Saionji, as for Mencius[2] and Zhu Xi, *ritsumei* meant taking charge of one's own life or destiny, taking responsibility for oneself and one's conduct of life, rather than blaming others (even Heaven) for whatever goes wrong or laying it to a malignant fate. Learning, understood primarily as the forming or shaping of a self into a responsible person, implied learning what one would be ready, in a given circumstance, to live by and stand for in both word and deed.

Another Meiji figure who shared this view, but better known as a writer and publicist than as an official or statesman, was Nakamura Masanao (Keiu, 1832–1890). An active contributor to the "Enlightenment" debates in the *Meiji Six Journal* (*Meiroku zasshi*),

Nakamura was distinctive among the promoters of the Enlightenment movement for his study of Neo-Confucianism under Satō Issai at the shogunal school, the Shōheikō. Satō reflected the late Tokugawa trend toward synthesis of Zhu Xi and Wang Yangming. Its strong emphasis on the morally responsible self and dedicated activism may help to explain why Nakamura was attracted to Protestant Christianity and became a translator of Samuel Smiles's *Self-Help* as well as of John Stuart Mills's *On Liberty*, both widely influential in promoting modern Western ideas in Meiji Japan.

No doubt still influenced by his early Neo-Confucian training, Nakamura saw many correspondences between Confucian tradition and the modern Western values he came to espouse. This contrasted with the thinking of Fukuzawa Yukichi in his early phase, whose advocacy of Western civilization, progress, and modernization implied a strong break with tradition. Thus the two were often seen as at opposite poles. Nakamura, though his familiarity with Western civilization was mostly with post-Reformation and Enlightenment movements in Europe, saw himself as basically looking for common human ground on which to reconcile Western traditions and Confucian values as a whole.

In a speech of April 1890 entitled "Past–Present, East–West: One Morality" he offered reflections on East–West values that can be taken as long-term tendencies predisposing him both to accept new ideas and to see in them confirmation of underlying human values common to China, Japan, and the West:

> In discussing similarities and differences among things, each is a distinct case. In comparing them, there is the objective of acknowledging the points they have in common—for example, when one says that even though men and women are different they are alike as humans, one speaks in recognition of the similarities. When one says that even though men and women are both human, still their natures differ in regard to firmness and softness, this is to acknowledge the differences. Thus, there are times when one acknowledges similarities using generalizations and synthesis, and other times when one recognizes differences using analysis. Even though, in teaching, a thousand similarities and ten thousand differences could be cited, in order to lead all people to the good, one emphasizes the similarities and talks in generalizations....
>
> What I will discuss today is the essential unity of East and West in basic morality.... In such a discussion there are times when one must

compare and analyze, and one cannot simply generalize. But today, my aim is to set aside small differences and stress large similarities, to do away with a narrow view and approach the large view of those of consummate achievement….

Moral virtue inheres in people naturally. It is a natural endowment from Heaven. From this naturally good knowledge and ability[3] in the people comes good conduct…. Therefore regardless of whether it is past or present, East or West, North or South, in all times, all places—this inherent moral virtue and basis of moral conduct, is common to all. There is overall great similarity and little difference [among humankind].

Nakamura then contrasts those universal human values with the seeming amorality of a view of evolution based on the survival of the fittest, but he rejects the idea that this latter view is necessarily characteristic of the West:

In this survival of the fittest situation, force becomes inevitable. It is as if morality and humaneness are being swept away like dust from the face of the earth and rather than emphasizing morality, people think they should display military might and assert themselves by force….

In the West, the individual (independent self) and sociality (human relations) are the two main pillars standing together. Around these two elements one's life is built. This sociality of human relations is a characteristic unique to mankind. We associate with others, sharing joys and sorrows, sharing fortune and misfortunes. Nevertheless this is secondary. The independent self within each person is the basis of morality, that is to say, the self is to be regarded as fundamental…. Since the choice of accepting or disregarding the good and evil in them is up to the freedom of each individual, the words or actions of the heart and mind all belong to the individual. Because they are based on the self, the responsibility for them also unavoidably reverts to the self. Again, response to or retribution for moral goodness or sin is something that returns to each individual. This then is the way of the principle of freedom….

As far as individual morality is concerned, regardless of past and present, East or West, in the end, the main principle is one thing called self-governance…. This self-governance, is, in other words, the central concern of the above-mentioned independent self and is the source of the principle of freedom (independence)…. In the above discussion, there is no freedom to be found apart from the moral person, and without freedom one is unable to choose goodness. Without freedom one cannot be resolute and at ease. To enlarge upon this discussion, [I will use the ideas of a] Western scholar who states that, this thing called freedom means to be the master of oneself. This closely resembles the earlier teaching in China that one should "be discriminating, keep to unity [what is common or shared] and hold to the Mean."[4] Moreover, this corresponds to the Song Confucian understanding which emphasized the Mind of the Way as master and the mind of man which is to obey Heaven's imperative [in the mind of the Way]....[5]

To sum this up in a few words, the true meaning of the Western philosophy of freedom, in Chinese terms, is to gain freedom by making the Mind of the Way [Heaven's principles] one's master and not being a slave to the human mind [conflicted by selfish desire]. This thing, freedom, is actually the basis of self-cultivation, that is, the root of self-governance. It is precisely in this that the origin of well-being lies as well as the foundation of family and state. This is one preeminent aspect of the view that the morality of past and present, East and West, is one.[6]

I have quoted Nakamura at some length here because as a progressive and "Westernizer" he feels the need to explain Western concepts of freedom and liberty in terms that are both central to Neo-Confucian teaching and distinctive of its own discourse. He seeks to translate prime Western and Chinese values in terms that are meaningful to each other, while also arguing for the need to sustain "Eastern," "Chinese," and Confucian studies as an important support for the freedom advocated in the West. When he speaks of "mastery of one's self" as the key, he is reiterating the fundamental point of Mencius, Zhu Xi, and Saionji concerning "taking charge of oneself" or "being master of one's fate." Even though the two formulations are not identical or equivalent, he sees essential common ground between them.

As between Saionji's Ritsumeikan and the later New Asia College of Tang Junyi and Qian Mu there are also obvious differences in the historical situation of each, but there is also common ground. When Nakamura feels compelled to defend Confucianism, to plead that Chinese culture not be abandoned, "not be despised" as he says,[7] in the Japanese rush to modernization, he reflects a sense of desperation over the threat to Confucianism's survival by wholesale Westernization in its adoptive homeland. Similarly, Tang and Qian, though taking refuge in Westernized Hong Kong, feel threatened by the loss of Confucian culture in both mainland China and the Western enclave on which it now depends for survival.

Today as well, the situation of Confucianism and the fate of the institutions Saionji, Qian, and Tang sought to establish, remain similarly precarious. In post–World War II Japan, going through its "miracle" of economic modernization, it has felt further pressures to globalize its educational system. The Ritsumeikan is no longer just a Confucian academy but a full-fledged Western-style university. In the early 1980s it became caught up in the fashionable trend toward what was called "internationalization" of the curriculum. As it happened I was doing research at Kyoto University, just after retiring as vice president for academic affairs at Columbia, and because of my involvement in curricular matters and educational planning, as well as what was thought of as "international studies," I was invited by the president of Ritsumeikan University to offer my advice on the "internationalization of the curriculum." Neither my host, nor a large assembly of faculty and students, would have been aware that at a conference sponsored by the U.S. Office of Education back in 1964, I had spoken in favor of using the National Defense Education Act to support humanistic studies of foreign cultures rather than emphasize geopolitical ones or defense-related military issues.[8] But when I addressed the topic of "the internationalization of the curriculum" at Ritsumeikan University, I led off by emphasizing that international studies (or what we would call globalization of the curriculum today) should be grounded first of all in the local culture, and native tradition should be understood as the proper soil for any organic growth reaching out to embrace other cultures or deal with the ongoing globalization of culture. To bring the point home, I asked my audience how, for instance, they would relate the current internationalization project to the original aims of Ritsumeikan's founders. What was their understanding of *ritsumei*? There was an embarrassed silence until finally a professor of Chinese classics gave an explanation based on Mencius (though with none of the Neo-Confucian nuances Saionji or Nakamura would have associated with it). No one else seemed to know.

This, I believe, is reflective of a widespread condition in East Asian universities today, which helps us to understand what is happening now in The Chinese University of Hong Kong, at a considerable remove from its founding as New Asia College, and how difficult it will be to "glocalize" as Professor Kwan hopes to do (i.e., not just to sustain local culture but actively to repossess and redevelop it) unless the process is coordinated with a globalization of the curriculum that itself supports glocalization.

What this means is that glocalization can succeed only if at the same time the globalized curriculum everywhere promotes the idea that a global education and global culture must be based on the concept of a developmental sequence in which globalization and glocalization reinforce each other. To some extent indeed this is already taking place. In Western countries where Asian classics have become available in general education to larger numbers of more broadly educated students, it is not uncommon for those exposed to the Asian classics in translation to develop an interest in the further study of the same texts and traditions in the original languages. The growth of Asian studies in the West has thus brought new reinforcements to the revival of interest in Asian traditions that have suffered severe attenuation in their homelands.

In this way the reading of Asian classics in translation, as part of general education in a core curriculum, can contribute to a globalization that helps to foster glocalization. And for this it is important that the work of translation proceed apace—that there be a continuing effort to produce accessible renditions. Indeed this would be true not only of translating more classic works but even of retranslating them. True classics are always subject to reinterpretation because they deal with pivotal issues always susceptible to reexamination and reinterpretation. The more central, the more deeply rooted in common human experiences, the more facets they expose to continuing reflection. The measure of a true classic is its incommensurability: of such a work there can be no "definitive translation," despite the frequent resort to this expression in common parlance.

Although enough translation had been done from Asian languages so that major works were already well known in nineteenth- and early-twentieth-century Europe and America and had long since stood as a challenging presence to leading Western writers and thinkers, more work needed to be done when the Asian Humanities program was launched at Columbia in 1948. This is because the work of translation from Asian traditions was far from complete or satisfactorily done for the purposes of general education. Sufficient translations of a reasonable quality were available to launch a worthwhile program, but there were many gaps, and there was also a major problem facing the extension of the program beyond a select few in an honors colloquium—the problem of translations suited to the general reader and accessible in forms not heavily burdened with scholarly annotation of the kind translators address primarily to specialists in their particular field of research.

Fortunately competent help was forthcoming in the persons of young scholars whose translations were to establish a new standard not only for scholarly excellence but for accessibility to students in general education. First of these was Donald Keene, whose *Anthology of Japanese Literature* (1955) made Japanese classic writings available in a convenient form at low cost—albeit at some cost also in the abridgment of works that would be better read as integral wholes. Keene proceeded to make up for this limitation of his *Anthology* by translating whole works only partly extracted in the earlier compilation. Most notable has been his translation of Kenkō's *Tsurezuregusa*, published under the title *Essays in Idleness* in the series of Translations from the Oriental Classics launched specifically to meet the needs of general education in what is now called the Asian Humanities. Next came Keene's *Major Plays of Chikamatsu*, and subsequently his translation of the drama *Chūshingura*. With the follow-up work done by Keene's students Royall Tyler and Karen Brazell, Keene's translations of Noh plays in his *Anthology* have been substantially supplemented by competent translations in inexpensive paperback editions. In the meantime another major work of classical Japanese literature, *The Pillow Book of Sei Shōnagon*, only excerpted in Keene's *Anthology*, was translated in whole by Ivan Morris, who was, before his untimely death, an active participant in the teaching of the Asian Humanities at Columbia. All of these classic works have thus become available in translations that in themselves have become standard works and virtual classics of the translator's art.

On the Chinese side, although many of the Chinese classics had been translated earlier, most notably by James Legge and Arthur Waley, and had been indispensable to the early offering of the course, many other Chinese works considered classic not only by the Chinese but by all East Asians remained untranslated or else were unavailable in a form suitable for student use. A major advance in this respect came through the translations of Wing-tsit Chan and Burton Watson from the Chinese of other classic works that convey the diversity and range of the Chinese—and what subsequently became the East Asian—tradition. Chan's translations of Laozi, Zhu Xi, and Wang Yangming are examples of such. Watson's early versions of alternative "classics" in Chinese antiquity—Mozi (Mo Tzu), Xunzi (Hsün Tzu), *Zhuangzi (Chuang Tzu)*, and Han Feizi—quickly made available by Columbia University Press in inexpensive paperbacks, became standard items on our Asian Humanities reading lists, and indeed set a new standard in the field for providing translations, both readable and reliable, for the general reader. Watson's wide range, versatility, and virtuosity as a translator have also been shown in his renderings of the *Records of the Grand Historian*, by Sima Qian (Ssu-ma Ch'ien), the *Vimalakirti* and *Lotus* sutras, and in his anthology of classic Chinese poetry, *The Columbia Book of Chinese Poetry*—all of which qualify for inclusion in our Asian Humanities reading list.

Our biggest challenge with regard to readable translations has come with the major texts of the Neo-Confucian tradition, which responded to the challenges of Buddhism and Daoism. The key texts are mostly in the form of Zhu Xi's commentaries on the Confucian classics, and commentaries make for more difficult reading than most of the original works themselves. For this reason many instructors prefer to avoid the Neo-Confucian texts in favor of more literary works (of which there is an almost unlimited supply). But these Neo-Confucian texts were the operative classics that shaped the later intellectual and ethical traditions of China, Japan, and Korea from the thirteenth to the twentieth centuries, and avoiding them is like ignoring everything in the West from Dante on. We have a similar problem with the medieval texts of the Islamic and Indian traditions, and it is not an easy dilemma to resolve, considering, as just one case in point, the lack of a suitable edition of a major work like Shankaracharya's commentaries on the *Brahma Sutras.* To some extent this deficiency can be made up for by using translated excerpts, for Shankara in the *Sources of Indian Tradition,* and for Zhu Xi, the new translations included in the second edition of the *Sources of Chinese Tradition.* Still, this is a compromise—better than nothing but less than satisfactory.

Further, on the Indian side the program has itself produced a major contributor to the translation of Indian thought and literature. Barbara Miller got her start as a Barnard undergraduate taking the

Asian Humanities course, went on into graduate studies in Sanskrit, and eventually produced translations, in a form ideally suited for the general reader, of important texts like the *Bhagavad Gita*, the *Shakuntala* of Kalidasa, *Love Song of the Dark Lord* (Gitagovinda), and the lyric poetry of Bhartrihari. Before her premature death, Barbara had established herself not only as a prime contributor to the Asian Humanities program but as a leading figure in the field of Indian and Sanskrit studies worldwide.

Thus it may be seen that while an Asian humanities program can rely on the inherent greatness of works that have established themselves over time—and through tough scrutiny and debate—as world classics, still their ability to "survive translation" (in Van Doren's terms) depends on having translators able to convey their contents in terms meaningful enough to new audiences in changing times and different cultures. And sometimes these new audiences prove to be Asians reading their own classics in translation.

Finally it is time to take up a question left open when I spoke above of translating, reading, or going back to "the original text." What does the "original text" actually mean or refer to? Modern scholarship has often cast doubt on the authorship, dating, and composition of texts once thought canonical. Sometimes that scholarship has succeeded in putting together a critical edition and at times such an edition has come to be accepted by a consensus of the scholarly community, wherefore our translators have generally respected that consensus in regard to the text (or texts) they choose to translate. But if the result of that critical process is a new text markedly different from the traditional one, there is a question whether, for all its historical or contextual relevance, the new version can be considered "classic." The conception of a humanities program based on the reading of classics or "great books" is that they have commanded the respect of generations and have survived a process of repeated scrutiny and contestation. We approach them initially on the recommendation of others, out of respect for the testimony others have given as to their greatness. Our willingness to make that effort is a measure, a gesture, of respect for what other human beings have experienced and valued—if only to the extent that they were challenged by these texts to come up with something better. The classics themselves then stand as monuments that commemorate the work of others—and obviously not just the leavings of "dead white boys." By reading them, we have access to a human dialogue that has withstood the test of time. We may listen in on that dialogue and join in to the extent that we make an effort to understand what they have most wanted to say to each other. It is an act of civility on our part, but now more than just a friendly gesture—it is an urgent necessity if civil discourse is to replace the new barbarism of the twenty-first century.

Notes

1. The Japanese sinologue Ogyū Sorai (1666–1728) raised similar objections to the translation of the Chinese classics into Japanese. See "Ogyū Sorai's Approach to Learning," in Wm. Theodore de Bary, Carol Gluck, and Arthur E. Tiedemann, eds., *Sources of Japanese Tradition*, vol. 2, *1600 to 2000*, 2nd ed. (New York: Columbia University Press, 2005), p. 280.

2. Mencius 7A1: "One who has fully developed his mind knows his nature. Knowing his nature, he knows Heaven. By preserving one's mind and nourishing one's nature one has the means to serve Heaven. When neither the brevity nor the length of a lifespan engenders doubts, and one cultivates one's person in an attitude of expectancy, one has the means to establish one's destiny" ("Selections from the *Mencius*," in Wm. Theodore de Bary and Irene Bloom, eds., *Sources of Chinese Tradition* [New York: Columbia University Press, 1999], vol. 1, p. 155).

3. See *Mencius* 7A:15.

4. Part of the "sixteen character formula" of Zhu Xi.

5. A reference to Zhu Xi's explanation of the sixteen-character formula in his preface to the *Mean*: "If one applies oneself to this without any interruption, making sure that the mind of the Way is the master of one's self and that the human mind always listens to its commands, then the precariousness and insecurity will yield to peace and security, and what is subtle and barely perceptible will become clearly manifest" ("Preface to the *Mean by Chapter and Phrase*," in de Bary and Bloom, eds., *Sources of Chinese Tradition*, vol. 1, pp. 732–733).

6. Nakamura Masanao, "Past–Present, East–West: One Morality," in de Bary, Gluck, and Tiedemann, eds., *Sources of Japanese Tradition*, vol. 2, pp. 769–775.

7. Nakamura Masanao, "Japan's Debt to China," in de Bary, Gluck, and Tiedemann, eds., *Sources of Japanese Tradition*, vol. 2, p. 718.

8. Wm. Theodore de Bary, "Education for a World Community," *Liberal Education, The Bulletin of the Association of American Colleges* 1, no. 4 (1964): 1–21.

4

Tang Junyi and the Philosophy of "General Education"

Cheung Chan Fai*

After the founding of New Asia College in 1949, Tang Junyi served as dean of the arts faculty and chair professor of the Department of Philosophy until his retirement in 1974. General education, though an integral part of the college curriculum, was never addressed as such in Tang's works. Nevertheless, he did write extensively on culture, education, and the interrelationship among the humanities, social sciences, and the natural sciences as academic disciplines, and placed great emphasis on the importance of humanistic education. Indeed, as one of the founders of the College, Tang must have taken part in drafting the mission statement and regulations of the College.[1] These are written in the spirit of the *shuyuan* of the Song dynasty academies. Number 14 of New Asia College regulations clearly states: "The college education of Sung Dynasty China is person-oriented, while modern college education is course-oriented. Our college spirit advocates completing person-orientation with various course programmes, teaching various courses with person-orientation."[2] In line with this view, regulation number 9 says, "Aspire to be an

CHEUNG Chan Fai is director of University General Education and professor in the Department of Philosophy, The Chinese University of Hong Kong.

Some of the ideas in this chapter have appeared in two earlier articles: "Humanities and Humanistic Education," *Humanities Bulletin* 2 (1993), and "The Idea of the Humanities," *Humanities Bulletin* 4 (1995).

all-rounder before aspiring to be an expert. To concentrate on the foundation of all-round knowledge is what is closest to your aptitude."[3] An emphasis on the education of the person rather than on mere acquisition of knowledge, as well as a preference for all-around knowledge to specialization, became the guiding principles of the College's General Education program.

Although indirect references do not constitute a philosophy of general education as such, I aim here to demonstrate the relevance of Tang's thinking on education and the idea of the humanities to the review and the restructuring of the present university general education program. This review was initiated in October 2002 by Vice-Chancellor, Professor Ambrose King, who was also head of New Asia College from 1977 to 1985. After nearly one year of consultation and discussion, the *Report of the Review Committee on General Education* (September 2003) was approved by the University Senate and the implementation of the new program was inaugurated in the academic year 2004/2005. Besides setting up a quality control mechanism for all existing university general education courses by a Standing Committee and external experts, the most important feature of the curriculum restructuring was the establishment of four areas of human concern that are not discipline specific. They are (1) Our Own Heritage; (2) Nature, Technology, and the Environment; (3) Society and Culture; and (4) Self and Humanity. All university general education courses were classified under these four categories and every undergraduate student was to take at least one course from each area in order to graduate.

Although there is no direct connection between Tang Junyi and this recent development of the university general education program, the new curriculum can be seen as the embodiment of the two essential characteristics of The Chinese University of Hong Kong, namely the liberal education of Chung Chi College and the humanistic tradition of New Asia College. Two of Tang's essays, "Human Learning and Human Existence" and "On the Distinction Between the Humanities, the Social Sciences, and the Natural Sciences,"[4] serve as important theoretical bases for the articulation of the four areas just named. To show their relevance, however, several ideas must first be clarified, namely the ideas of the university, the humanities, liberal education, and general education.

The Idea of a University

Though New Asia College joined the Chinese University in 1963, Tang did not fully accept the organization and the administration of the University. Because of its advantages for the college graduates Tang agreed that the College should become a part of the federal university, but he did so reluctantly because he saw the mission of New Asia College as different from other colleges. Time and again, he stressed the aim of the College as succeeding to the spirit of the Song–Ming *shuyuan*. Hence New Asia College was and is called a *shuyuan* and not, like Chung Chi College, a *xueyuan*, the origin of which is clearly Western European. The inheritance and development of Chinese culture are the main aims of the College. This was a task with a heavy cultural responsibility against the background of the crisis of Chinese culture in Communist China. Tang and other Confucian scholars regarded the total collapse of Chinese traditional culture as imminent. New Asia College was one of the last hopes for rescuing Chinese culture. In his mind, New Asia College was to be the *Chinese* university writ large. The academic disciplines should focus primarily on Chinese culture.[5] Such ideas are called the New Asia Spirit. The central idea of this humanistic education was to combine study and life. The very first regulation states: "Put equal emphasis on the advancing of one's studies and the conduct of oneself; better still to achieve a combined mastery of both."[6] In "The Past, Present, and Future of New Asia," one of his last lectures before retirement, Tang reiterated the Chinese humanistic ideal of New Asia on the one hand and pointed out the crisis in university education on the other hand. The fragmentation of academic disciplines, the instrumental purpose of degree programs, the alienation of learning from living as well as of teachers from students are the major problems challenging the ideal of New Asia.[7] The ultimate goal was to rescue Chinese culture through academic learning. He firmly believed that "if the spirit of Chinese culture, which is potentially in the mind of the Chinese people, can be developed, China is certain to be rejuvenated."[8]

Yet the idea of the *shuyuan*, with all its stress on a high degree of moral and cultural responsibility, seemed to be too idealistic for Hong Kong. With the establishment of the Chinese University in 1963, the autonomy of each constituent college over academic matters was gradually surrendered to the central administration. Tang openly expressed regret over this and felt betrayed by the University.[9] The disagreement between Tang and the Chinese University came to a climax when Tang resigned from the University Council in 1976 and, subsequently, with the withdrawal of the New Asia College Graduate School from the Chinese University. The tension, I believe, lay not only in the difference in political and administrative judgment but also in the very conception of a university. After all, the spirit of the *shuyuan* may not be in complete harmony with the modern university.

The university is indeed a Western concept. The modern idea of the university originated in twelfth-century Europe. The Latin idea of *universitas*, or *studium generale*, means *magistrorum et scholarum*, a community of scholars and students in teaching and learning. Hence *collegium*, college in the modern sense, has more or less the same meaning. The classical universities, like those of Paris and Bologna, were established out of professional and utilitarian motives. There were four professional faculties, namely law, medicine, theology, and philosophy, organized and administered by members of the professional guilds. The aims of the classical university were to fulfill the demands of society. The universities "emerged to meet the overwhelming need to provide for the training of lawyers, schoolmasters and clerics to fill the ranks of the increasingly sophisticated administrations of both church and state."[10] This classical idea of the university is clearly in contradistinction to the Chinese *shuyuan*, which emphasized the moral transformation of oneself without regard to any practical concern. Perhaps there was one thing shared by the *shuyuan* and *universitas*: the idea of *studium generale*; that is, the students of these educational institutes came from various parts of the country. They came together to join scholars in learning and studying. This trans-provincial or even international character is still the essential feature of the university today.

The modern conception of the university as a higher institute of teaching, learning, and research was a product of nineteenth-century England and Germany. It was Cardinal Newman and Wilhelm von Humboldt who set the common goals of the university. Newman regarded liberal education, inherited primarily from Aristotle, as the central role of the university, whereas von Humboldt focused on academic integrity and freedom to teach, to learn, and to do research.[11] In fact, the prevailing idea of the contemporary research university stems more from von Humboldt than from Newman. The elitism of a gentlemanly education as expounded by Newman was severely criticized by those who demanded a democratization of university education. The university should be open to all and not be the privilege of a certain class of people.

Certainly, the debate on the meaning and aim of the university is still very much alive in our contemporary world. What is relevant to my discussion of general education in relation to Tang Junyi's philosophy is the changing situation of Hong Kong and China. The urgency of the crisis in Chinese culture is no longer the focus of discussion. The scholars exiled from China are now seen as just historical figures. Their concern for a humanistic education in the university has been largely ignored. Though the New Asia College regulations are still printed in every annual edition of the college handbook, I wonder who ever cares to read and study them seriously. These are only idealistic records of the past.

What is then the meaning of the university? What role can general education play? Is there any relevance of Tang's philosophy to our present university education?

The Present Crisis of University Education in Hong Kong

The 2002 report on "Higher Education in Hong Kong" by the University Grants Commission states clearly that the major purpose of higher education is to ensure the economic development of Hong Kong. Recognizing the inevitability of the advent of a knowledge-based economy, the report claims: "That knowledge-based economy is at the core of Hong Kong SAR's future economic development. Without a highly educated and capable workforce, with the necessary developmental skills, there will be no success in building a knowledge economy, which is not simply appropriate for, but is essential to, Hong Kong's place as a developed, internationally focused community."[12]

Indeed, this statement of purpose is only an echo and a reinforcement of what the last British Hong Kong government had laid down for the aim of higher education a few years before. The UPGC report stated: "The purpose of investing in world-class higher education institutions in Hong Kong is to improve the *economic performance* of Hong Kong itself, but the existence of such institutions and the opportunities which they would offer, particularly in such areas as *technology transfer*, would undoubtedly be of benefit to the *hinterland* as well."[13]

The economic prosperity of Hong Kong and China is the primary goal of university education in Hong Kong. Hence it is no wonder that the main recommendations of the report are the reallocation of funds, governance, and management of higher education. In short, the meaning of the university lies in its functional and market values. Hence the professionalization, specialization, and vocationalism of the university curriculum and the compartmentalization of the administrative structure are all justified to this end. Students are receiving training in specified realms of knowledge in order to perform their respective services to society, be they accounting, education, engineering, medicine, or law, depending on the needs and demands; while professors are expected to deliver the required updated knowledge and skills to the students. Their research activities should also be confined to these functions. To put it bluntly: the university is an institution that preserves, disseminates, and develops a commodity called knowledge through lectures and research by professors to the students for the sake of serving the needs of society.[14]

The utilitarian functions and professional ends of the university are now taken for granted. The emphasis on quantitative and qualitative control over academia is to ensure the optimal productivity of the university to face the challenges of our society for the so-called knowledge-based economy. Indeed, university education is a most expensive investment and the demand for cost/ benefit return is therefore seen as completely legitimate and well justified. However, this is exactly what Jackson Lears named as the chief threat to "intellectual freedom in the academy." He further elaborates: "The main menace is market-driven managerial influence: the impulse to subject universities to quantitative standards of efficiency and productivity, to turn knowledge into a commodity, to transform open sites of inquiry into corporate research laboratories and job training centers."[15]

To run the university as a commercial business and to teach knowledge as a product are the two major operations of the mercantilism that is implicit in the present policy of higher education. If mercantilism is really the underlying ideology, then what is the purpose of discussing the idea of the university anymore? If the knowledge-based economy is our inevitable predicament, then what is the point in asserting the pursuit of knowledge beyond utilitarian motives as the ideal of learning? Is there a need anymore to promote the broad, nonspecialized, and apparently useless general education program?

I do not think mercantilism and utilitarianism are wrong. I do agree with the utilitarian demand on the university. But I believe there is more in university education than just mercantilism. The university should be more than a service industry writ large. Of course our world has been changed drastically in the last century. There are different challenges for the modern university: massification, vocationalism, globalization, and internationalization are issues that appear only in the contemporary world. Consequently the meaning of "university" should also be changed. That higher education should be accountable for the need of society has become a fact.

I may have oversimplified and exaggerated the situation. Yet it is my fear that the classical ideal of the university has completely disappeared. There is almost no place for any discussion of the spirit of the *shuyuan*. Indeed, the elite concept of the traditional university has been secularized in the last century to become one of a mass university. The intellectual pursuit of knowledge for its own sake, though it used to be the traditional mission of the university, has nearly lost its meaning. Although it seems to be naive or just romantic to talk about the meaning and the ideal of the university, it is still necessary to recall once again the idea of the university in order to reexamine the meaning of teaching and learning. I believe a philosophical and historical rethinking of the ideas of the university, the humanities, general education, teaching, and learning is therefore not a futile mental exercise after all.

The Idea of the Humanities

The idea of the humanities comes from the classical tradition of Western culture. It has its root in the Greek idea of *paideia* and was later a derivative of the Latin *humanitas*. It was further incorporated in the *studia humanitatis* by the humanists in the Renaissance. The humanities are considered both as the ideal of man and as the curriculum for ideal education. The purpose of *studia humanitatis* is to educate oneself to become a free person and a good citizen. In short the idea of the humanities is closely related to Western cultural history and the Western ideal of education. On the other hand, the Chinese concept of humanities (*renwen*) originated in the *Yi Jing* and was later incorporated into the educational ideal of Confucianism. "To observe movements in Heaven (*tienwen*) so as to understand the change in time; to observe human activities (*renwen*) so as to acculturate the world." The human activities mentioned here are not simply any human activities but a special set of moral activities. Tang Junyi explains: "The term *renwen* in Chinese stresses the idea of man [*ren*] rather than external activities [*wen*]. It demands the self-awareness of man as man and the conscious recognition of the immanent moral virtues, only through which can man achieve his authentic self."[16] This agrees with the traditional dominant Confucian doctrine of education, of which the aim is to actualize one's moral virtues and to extend these moral activities to the world.

Tang Junyi has written extensively on Chinese and Western humanisms and their relationship to education. Accordingly, his major concerns are the philosophical justification of the classification of knowledge and the status of man within the universe of knowledge. His essay on the distinction between the humanities, the social sciences and the natural sciences is perhaps the only Chinese work on this topic. According to Tang, all branches of knowledge originate from human subjectivity. The difference between the humanities and other sciences does not lie in the different subject matters of study. In a certain sense, all positive sciences (i.e., disciplines) imply each other. Take historical science as an example; no one will disagree that all knowledge is historical in nature. Physical knowledge, so fixated in a text of linguistic symbols, is a historical text. The difference lies in the ways in which human beings see the world. Tang explains:

> The difference between the natural sciences, social sciences, and the humanities lies in the three major attitudes or perspectives from which human beings view the world. The first perspective is to see things and events that are separated or external to my subjective experience and thought. Those things and events are assumed to exist independently, hence the emergence of the natural sciences. The second perspective is

to see myself as part of the human community. My subjective experience and thought are objectivized as part of those of the community. The interrelationship between the experience and thought of each member, that is, the foundation of the community, then becomes the basis of the social sciences. The third is to include my subjective experience and thought together with the experience and thought of nature and of community, in order to locate them in the realm of my subjectivity, and to reflect consciously the interrelationship between them. This is the foundation of the humanities.[17]

Since my main interest is in Tang's idea of the humanities, his view on the natural and social sciences will not be considered in detail here. Tang thinks that there are three subject matters of the humanities: events (*shi*), sentiments (*qing*), and principles (*li*). Events are one's experience of nature and community. They are themselves not material things but are sedimented in one's consciousness as memory. As the memory of these events can be recalled in the form of linguistic symbols, and if they are so recollected and rearranged according to the objective time order, they are elements of history. On the other hand, one could have one's sentimental reaction toward these events that could further be dissociated from their respective objective time order and be expressed in a special linguistic form. This is the origin of the literary arts. However, if one reflects on the reason and meaning of the events and sentiments, then attention is now paid to the principles pertinent to these events and sentiments. To reflect the principles is the task of philosophy. Furthermore, events, sentiments, and principles are mutually generative. The principles of events engender philosophy; and this philosophy in turn becomes an event that can be the subject matter of a history of philosophy; and finally the principles of history can be understood from a philosophical perspective, hence a philosophy of history.

Tang's thesis is far more complex than what I have outlined above. His language is sometimes dense and very obscure. For purposes of this paper it is perhaps enough to understand the basic tenets of his idea of the humanities. What Tang wants to do is to give a philosophical interpretation of the classical Chinese conception of the humanities: literature, history, and philosophy, which are mutually interrelated and form a unity of study. No discipline of the humanities can ever be a truly independent study without making reference to the other two studies. The foundation of the humanities lies in human subjectivity and reflective activities. At the same time, there is a close relationship between the humanities and other sciences. In another article, Tang tries to demonstrate that all knowledge is indeed rooted in human existence.[18] He asserts that no knowledge can exist independently from human existence. This is clearly a humanistic interpretation of knowledge to the extent that the humanities take priority over all other areas of knowledge.

According to Tang, the primacy of the value of human existence in knowledge is an answer to the compartmentalization and alienation of academic study in the present world. The search for knowledge cannot be value free. Against the Aristotelian idea of knowledge for its own sake, Tang extols humanistic education with reference to general and specialized education. Indeed, the idea of "general" in this context means "all-around." The mission statement of New Asia College of 1950 states:

> Only through humanistic education can the ills of the educational environment, in which knowledge for individual vocational purposes and studies, as well as the seeking of knowledge for the sake of knowledge in the guise of doctorate or scholastic style, be saved. Based on the above intentions, all curricula of this college place primary emphasis on all-around knowledge [general education], and then the pursuit of specialization. Basic training of literary skills comes first and then courses on common issues of human existence and culture, so as to establish a good foundation on a broad basis, and only then to develop various special disciplines and skills according to the different aptitude of each individual student. The purpose is to let the student have authentic understanding of his/her own special ability in relation to his/her role and meaning in the academic world as well as in life. This is the remedy for the errors of academic indifference and fragmentation that result from the separation of faculties, disciplines, and departments in the contemporary university.[19]

This statement was published some fifty years ago, but it still has relevance to our university education, though it is not referred to by Tang. The term "general education" is not mentioned, no doubt because it was still uncommon at that time, but whether it serves the same purposes as "general education" depends on what is meant by that term.

The Idea of General Education

Robert Hutchins, the architect of the general education program at Chicago, referred to general education as a "common stock of fundamental ideas" that is essential for a university. He says: "Unless students and professors (and particular professors) have a common intellectual training, a university must remain a series of disparate schools and departments, united by nothing except the fact that they have the same president and board of trustees."[20] General education is accordingly the common stock of intellectual concerns shared by students and professors.

General education as a contemporary invention of American universities has no counterpart in European universities, past or present. Moreover, it has never been shown that those universities with general education programs are better than those without. Nor has the meaning and the content of general education been fully agreed upon by scholars and educators.[21] Nevertheless, there is a common reason underlying the establishment of general education in American universities. The various programs of general education, like the Core Curriculum at Columbia and Harvard, the General Education Program of Chicago, are reactions to the overspecialization and professionalization of the undergraduate curricula at Columbia and Chicago, and then at Harvard after World War II. Specialization breeds intellectual provincialism and dogmatism, whereas professionalization emphasizes only the instrumental values of knowledge. A narrow-minded professional, who might be very successful in his own field, is nevertheless not considered to be an educated and cultured person. What is involved here is the recurrent belief of the classical ideals of *paideia* and *humanitas*; the belief that before a person becomes professional he must first be educated as a human being. In this respect, general education derives in fact from the liberal education tradition.

In this sense, Tang Junyi and the founders of New Asia College share a common belief in liberal and general education with Western scholars. Tang's humanistic education means more or less the same as the original humanities program at Columbia and the later general education programs at Chicago and Harvard.

Humanistic Education and General Education

The intention of this paper is to show a connection between Tang Junyi's philosophy and the present curriculum restructuring of general education at The Chinese University of Hong Kong, which arose from the somewhat chaotic situation of the general education program in the last decade. With more than two hundred courses offered by nearly forty academic departments participating in the program, there has been a lack of direction and rationale in the program as a whole. Professors and students have taken part in this required curriculum without knowing the reason for it. Hence general education has sometimes been considered a useless appendage to the major study. This lack of a coherent structure and an inadequate governance system finally called for a comprehensive review.

The established areas of study, mentioned in the first paragraphs of this paper, are the result of an attempt to bring back basic humanistic ideas into the university curriculum. Unlike many general education programs offered locally or in the United States, these areas are not divided according to discipline. We recognize the distinctive autonomy of each academic discipline. But the classical meaning of general education, *studium generale*, points to the teaching and learning within a community of scholars and students. "General" does not mean ordinary, but "all" and "common." Hence general education means a common education for all and by all constituents of the university. General education courses should not be electives of each discipline, but they should be designed by professors in a particular discipline for students from other departments without any prerequisite. With Tang's idea of humanistic education in mind, the four areas are conceived in terms of the fundamental intellectual concern of our existence: we should know our own cultural heritage and our relation to nature, society, and ourselves in order to be human beings capable of self-awareness and reflection. The four areas are[22]

1. *Our own heritage*: Students of the Chinese University should have a basic knowledge of our Chinese cultural heritage and have a comprehensive understanding of the essential characteristics of Chinese civilization. Students should learn to appreciate and evaluate, by way of an integrated approach,

their own cultural heritage from a broad historical, social, and intellectual perspective.

2. *Nature, technology, and the environment*: The courses should introduce students to an understanding of nature, science, and technology, our role as part of nature, the effect of human activities on the environment, the impact of science and technology on life and society, and the implications of these for the future of humankind.

3. *Society and culture*: Courses should enhance understanding of the ways in which human societies and cultures are formed and represented in their generality as well as in their diversity. These courses should also introduce students to the theories and/or methodologies through which social, political, economic, or cultural issues are studied.

4. *Self and humanity*: This area aims to explore the diversity of values and the meaning of human endeavors, and to enhance students' understanding of self through the study of the humanities and related disciplines.

Though Tang never formulated a philosophy of general education as such, we hope this new general education program can be truly in the spirit of his ideals of humanistic education. In this way the original spirit of New Asia College can be rejuvenated and institutionalized in our university curriculum.

Notes

1. Qian Mu was probably the main author of the regulations in 1950. See Qian-Mu, "Zong Xinya shuyuan Han Qian Mu xianshang de jiaoyu sixiang," in Zhu Hanmin and Li Hongqi, eds., *Zhongguo shuyuan* (Changsha: Hunan jiaoyu chubanshe, 1997).

2. The New Asia College Regulations in *New Asia College Handbook*, 2004–2005, p. 101. No such regulation was prescribed for the other constituent colleges. It is clearly a modern adaptation of Zhu Xi's "Articles of the White Deer Grotto Academy," in Wm. Theodore de Bary and Irene Bloom, eds., *Sources of Chinese Tradition*, 2nd ed. (New York: Columbia University Press, 1999), vol. 1, pp. 742–744.

3. New Asia College Regulations, no. 9, p. 100.

4. Tang Junyi, *Zhonghua renwen yu dangjin shejie* (Taibei: Xuesheng shuju, 1975).

5. Tang Junyi, "Dui weilai jiaoyu fangzhen de zhanwang," in Xin Ya yan jiu suo, ed., *Xinya jiaoyu* (Hong Kong: Xin Ya yan jiu suo, 1981), pp. 131–134, reprinted from *Xin Ya sheng huo Shuang Zhou Kan* 1, no. 17 (1960): 1–2.

6. New Asia College Regulations, no. 1, p. 100.

7. Tang Junyi, "Xinya de guoyu, xianzai yu jianglai," in *Xinya xiao kan* (1973; reprint, Hong Kong: Xin Ya yan jiu suo, 1981), pp. 151–165.

8. Tang Junyi, "Wo suo liaojie zhi Xinya jing sheng," in *Xin Ya xiao kan* (Hong Kong: Xin ya shu yuan, 1952), p. 2.

9. Tang Junyi, "Xinya de Guoyu ya jianglai," in *Xinya jiaoya*, p. 156.

10. James Bowen, *A History of Western Education* (London: Methuen, 1975), vol. 2, p. 103.

11. For a more elaborated discussion on the idea of the university, see Cheung Chan Fai, "Tongshi jiaoyu daxue linian," in Lai Chi Tim, Lau Kwok Ying, and Cheung Chan Fai, eds., *Zaiqiu zhende daolu shang* (Hong Kong: Zhonghua shuju, 2003), pp. 265–281.

12. Stewart R. Sutherland, *Higher Education in Hong Kong: Report of the University Grants Commission* (Hong Kong: University Grants Commission, 2002), p. 4.

13. Hong Kong University and Polytechnic Grants Committee, *Higher Education, 1991–2001: An Interim Report* (Hong Kong: Government Printer, 1993), p. 9 (my italics).

14. The mission and vision of The Chinese University of Hong Kong echo precisely this idea: "Our Mission: To assist in the preservation, creation, application and dissemination of knowledge by teaching, research and public service in a comprehensive range of disciplines, thereby serving the needs and enhancing the well-being of the citizens of Hong Kong, China as a whole, and the wider world community. Our Vision: To be acknowledged locally, nationally and internationally as a first-class comprehensive research university whose bilingual and multicultural dimensions of student education, scholarly output and contribution to the community consistently meet standards of excellence" (*Calendar/The Chinese University of Hong Kong, 2004–2005* [Hong Kong: Chinese University of Hong Kong, 2004], p. iii).

15. Jackson Lears, "The Radicalism of Tradition: Teaching the Liberal Arts in a Managerial Age," *Hedgehog Review* 2 (2000): 8.

16. Tang Junyi, *Zhongguo renwen jingshen zhi fadian* (Taibei: Xuesheng shuju, 1974), p. 21

17. Tang Junyi, *Zhongguo renwen yu dangjin shejie* (Taibei: Xuesheng shuju, 1975), pp. 185–186.

18. Tang Junyi, "Ren de xuewen yu ren de cunzai," in *Zhongguo renwen yu dangjin shejie*, pp. 65–109.

19. Qian Mu, *Xinya yi do* (Taibei: Dongda tushu gongsi, 1989), pp. 3–4 (my translation).

20. Robert Maynard Hutchins, *The Higher Learning in America* (1936; New Brunswick, N.J.: Transaction, 1995), p. 59.

21. Ernst L. Boyer and Arthur Levine, *A Quest for Common Learning: The Aims of General Education* (Stanford, Calif.: Carnegie Foundation for the Advancement of Teaching, 1981), especially appendix A, "Historical Purposes of General Education," where fifty different purposes are listed.

22. The following description of the four areas is a free rendition of the text from the Review Committee on General Education, "Report of the Review Committee on General Education," chap. 4, p. 1.

5

The Overdominance of English in Global Education

A Glocal Response

Kwan Tze-wan

In the course of human history, language has played a remarkably important role. Intellectually speaking, language constitutes the core of the mental activities of humankind. It is the formative force of human consciousness and culture, and the means of individual expression and interpersonal communication. As a social institution, language unites as well as divides, integrates as well as segregates. Language has much to do with the identity and solidarity of a people; it is at once the subject matter and the carrier of cultural traditions. On the other hand, languages compete with each other and can be a source of conflict. In the age of globalization, these aspects of

KWAN Tze-wan is director of Research Centre for Humanities Computing and Archive for Phenomenology & Contemporary History, and professor in the Department of Philosophy, The Chinese University of Hong Kong.

This chapter is a slightly abridged version of a paper presented at the Ninth East–West Philosophers' Conference, Educations and Their Purposes: A Philosophical Dialogue Among Cultures, held May 29–June 10, 2005, at the East–West Center, University of Hawai'i at Manoa, Honolulu. The paper is included in this book with the consent of Professor Roger Ames, convener of the conference. Also with the consent of Professor Ames, the original version of the paper, with more elaborate discussion on Leibniz's reflections on the German language of his time and with more notes, will appear in the collection *Phenomenology 2005*, to be published electronically by the Organization of Phenomenological Organizations.

language have become more complex than ever with the rise of English as a truly global language.

Historically speaking, mankind has witnessed the coming and going of many lingua francas that flourished in different times and in different geographical areas. In the West, there was Greek in antiquity, Latin in the Middle Ages, and French and to some extent German in modern times. In the East, there was Chinese, especially in its written form. In Africa, there was Swahili and in South America Quechua and Spanish, to mention just the most prominent examples. However, in terms of scope and impact, it seems that it is English that has become the first truly global lingua franca,[1] "global" not merely in a geographical sense but in the sense that the spread of English has become an inseparable part of what we now call globalization. It is for this reason that Philipson and Skutnabb-Kangas, two prominent scholars in research on linguistic human rights, have coined the term "englishization," which they define as "one dimension of globalization."[2]

From a pragmatic point of view, the world has always been in need of a lingua franca. In fact the term *lingua franca*, originally referring to the language of the Franks (Europeans), was invented in the European Middle Ages, when there was a need for different peoples in the Mediterranean region and throughout the Middle East to have a common language that could be used "freely" to facilitate multilateral trade, diplomacy, and to some extent scholarly exchange. In our globalized world today, the urgency of the need for international communication has reached an unprecedented level. Think of the various world/regional economic summits, of organizations such as the United Nations or UNESCO, of the multitudes of international academic conferences held from day to day around the globe. Nowadays, peoples of the world can hardly afford to disregard the importance of English, in whatever walk of life, if they do not want to be marginalized by the global community.

Dominance versus *Over*dominance

Language is power. This much-expressed dictum takes on a new meaning with the upsurge of English as a global language. Like many lingua francas in history, including Greek and Latin, the power of English was first backed up by military and economic force. In addition, the power of English has a significant bearing on the social level as well. Whether we like it or not, proficiency in English has become in many societies not only a matter of practical competence but also a yardstick of social prestige, or "cultural capital," as depicted by Bourdieu.[3] Finally, the power of English expanded greatly when English became the most important carrier of new knowledge.[4] It is also through this means that the dominance of English poses a challenge to global education. Whoever wants to be well informed, whoever wants to be globally heard or read, finds reading or publishing in English a necessity.

Yet, while this dominance of English is today unavoidable, the world is now facing an additional challenge—the *over*dominance of English. By overdominance of English, I mean the danger of individual languages being self-estranged through an overemphasis on English at the cost of the mother tongue. While dominance is an externally imposed challenge, overdominance is largely a self-inflicted endangerment of the mother tongue through a kind of self-neglect and self-degradation by people of various linguistic communities. In education, one serious consequence of the overdominance of English is the "crowding out"[5] of the native tongue from school curricula and from higher education, a scenario that is not uncommon around the globe today.

One reason we need to draw a distinction between the dominance and overdominance of English is that the two issues allow for different sorts of reactions. As a result of globalization, the dominance of English is a brute fact that some nations are benefiting from and others have to tolerate. It is a global issue that is now under the direct control of no nation. As a danger to native languages, however, the overdominance of English is a matter of domestic language policies or attitudes, which are but under the control of members of the respective linguistic communities, whether government policy makers, university administrators, or the general public. The present paper seeks to stimulate reflection on, and constructive responses to, this problem.

The Experience of Germany Through Four Centuries

To exemplify how far-reaching the problem of overdominance can become, let us examine the experience of the Germans. In terms of influence, the German language was at its prime probably for the whole of the nineteenth century, reaching its pinnacle just before the outbreak of World War I. During that period, German was the most important scholarly language for academic disciplines ranging from astrophysics to art history, from mathematics to sociology, and from economics to philosophy. But before and after this heyday, the situation was quite different.

Although a language with a traceable history, German was in the time of Leibniz and Bach very much neglected, not merely internationally, but by Germans themselves. One remarkable story is that of Frederick the Great, who, when introduced to J. S. Bach, tried to speak to him in French. Another story relates that Voltaire felt so at home in the Prussian court that he wrote to his countrymen, saying, "It is just like in France, people here just speak our language, German is used only when they are talking to soldiers and horses." And this *schwarmerei* for French was not confined to the royals or nobles alone. Peter von Polenz, a famous historian of German, tells us that, at the turn of the eighteenth century, it was common for middle class German families to require their children to speak French to their parents and to their friends, while German was spoken only to the helpers or maids.[6] In academia, German had at that time a very low status. We only need to recall that most of Leibniz's own writings were either in Latin or in French, the two leading lingua francas at that time.

But the most interesting thing about Leibniz was that he did write a few short essays in German, two of which dealt precisely with the future prospect of German as an academic language. The titles of the two essays are as follows:[7]

1. "Unvorgreifliche Gedanken, betreffend die Ausübung und Verbesserung der deutschen Sprache" [Some unanticipated thoughts concerning the practice and improvement of the German language] (1697/1704/1709)
2. "Ermahnung an die Deutschen, ihren Verstand und ihre Sprache besser zu üben, samt beigefügtem Vorschlag einer deutschgesinnten Gesellschaft" [Warning to the Germans, to better exercise their understanding and their language, together with a proposal for a German-minded society] (1682/1683)

In these two essays, and in some related correspondence, Leibniz brought forth two important notions related to the use of the German language, namely *Sprachpflege* (language care) and *deutschgesinnte Gesellschaft* (German-minded society). The concept of language care is quite akin to the concept of language planning (*Sprachplanung*), for both concepts suggest that we should take measures regarding our native language so that it may develop in a favorable direction. The difference is that language planning is more or less a matter of governmental policy, whereas language care has to do mainly with the duty of members of the linguistic community. And Leibniz's idea of a German-minded society[8] refers precisely to this need of "caring" for the German language[9] through its active use by the German people so that the strength and vitality of the language may develop and prosper.

According to Leibniz, German exhibited its strength in having a rich vocabulary for sensible and technical objects (metallurgy, mining, etc.), but suffered from a shortfall in terminology in two specific areas—that of "the expression of the emotions" and that of "abstract and subtle cognitive expressions, including those used in logic and metaphysics." In other words, Leibniz thought German was weak in the areas of literature and philosophy.[10]

For today's admirers of German culture, this "diagnosis" of Leibniz is hardly comprehensible. In fact, by taking a closer look at the history of the German language, it is not hard for us to discover that it was precisely in the two specified areas that the track record of the German language up to Leibniz's time was indeed not a bad one. There was a long tradition of medieval and baroque German poetry on the one hand and an equally remarkable tradition of German schoolmen and mystics on the other.[11] Therefore, Leibniz's assessment of the German language was arguably the result of his underestimation of his own linguistic heritage. And the fact that an academic as serious as Leibniz could also take such a view seems to indicate clearly that the German people of his time, with few exceptions, must have lost confidence and esteem in their own language and must have given up on its "care" to the extent that they could even have become unaware of its previous glamour. In any case, with the proposal of the concepts of "language care" and of a "German-minded society," Leibniz did point to the direction along which the German language might experience a resurrection.

Within a hundred years after Leibniz's "warning," the German language eventually did make enormous progress in both literature and philosophy. In the hands of such literati as Goethe and Schiller and such philosophers as Kant and Hegel, the German language experienced a kind of rebirth. Through the work of these intellectual giants, the German language reclaimed all its lost territory, becoming one of the most powerful and expressive academic languages of modern Europe.

After another century of development, the power of German reached its climax just before World War I. With the rapid rise of English during the interwar period, however, the influence of German was significantly checked, and during and after World War II, German suffered further due to the negative image and inhumane deeds of the Nazis.[12] Culturally and politically, the situation in present-day Germany is very similar to the Germany of Leibniz's lifetime: First, the Holy Roman Empire's significant weakness for some fifty years following the Thirty Years' War (1618–1648) finds a parallel in the overhang felt in present-day Germany of the country's defeat in World War II some fifty years ago. Second, while Leibniz's Germany came under the Western influence of the language of France, the final winner of the Thirty Years' War, the same sort of "West influence" is felt by today's Germany, the difference being that this time the West wind comes not from France but from the further shores of the United States. With the upsurge of English (or better, American English), the future of the German language, which once burdened Leibniz, seems to have become a matter for alarm again.

Out of their great concern for this issue, a group of German university professors (thirty-seven in number) wrote an open letter on June 24, 2001, addressed to the Ministers of Culture, of Science, and of Education of all sixteen German states.[13] This open letter bears the caption "Protection and Development of German as National Academic Language." In this letter, the authors brought the world's attention to two noticeable trends regarding the usage of German on German soil: First, an increasing number of international conferences in Germany are using English as the only official language, even when the main target audience is German laypeople. Second, an increasing number of publications in Germany accept only English contributions, and many basic university courses are now offered in English rather than in German.

Seeing the gravity of the issue, the authors made the alarming statement that "the three undersigned together with the thirty-four countersigned, coming from the most disparate disciplines, observe with great concern how the German language is being expelled from our country's academic enterprise by English. We most politely ask you to take issue with this problem. We also recognize the danger that the primordial language basis for our scientific thinking and for our social exchange of knowledge will be lost within the next five to ten years. This applies also to the significance of Germany as an independent country for academic research." In the face of such a danger, the open letter suggested a number of measures to be taken, which include (1) political initiatives (following the example of France) toward designating German, in conjunction with English, the official language of international conferences held in Germany; (2) using public money to translate specially compiled research materials into German to facilitate public access; and (3) ensuring that course offerings in German in university undergraduate programs are not heedlessly suppressed in favor of English.

Looking back at the heyday of Goethe and Kant, when the German language was so alive, it is hard to imagine that the same language now faces such a decline. Putting the whole case in Leibniz's words, what the open letter was complaining about was nothing but the Germans' own abandonment of "language care," which is precisely what should again be strengthened. What if the suggested measures are not followed? Of course, with so many speakers the German language will not easily die out. But it would be bad enough, as depicted in the open letter, if German higher education were to produce a class of isolated elite cut off from the rest of society and incapable of using German in academic writing, discussion, or even thinking![14]

How Should the Overdominance of English Be Dealt With?

The above trajectory of the German language shows us clearly what challenges the globalization of English might entail for all other national languages. With the experience gained from this account, I will proceed to reflect on a number of topics in the hope that some key issues can be identified and clarified so that peoples in the world may deal with the same problem in a more deliberate manner. In presenting an argument that is of practical relevance, I will unavoidably have to occasionally proceed from a "Chinese" perspective. This is necessary, as there are indications showing that major universities in China and in Hong Kong have considered or are considering major revisions of their language policy in favor of English. But I hope this "Chinese" perspective will not prevent us from seeing that what we are facing here is a challenge that the whole world is also facing. Given the global nature of this challenge, which inevitably will intensify in the time to come, some generic reflections might already be timely.

1. *English as the indispensable key to the global community*: After decades of self-seclusion, the opening up of China has become an issue of paramount importance both for the Chinese as well as for would-be partners. Propelled by the enormous opportunities that lie ahead for those who can communicate with people from outside China, it is perfectly understandable that a great interest has arisen among the Chinese population in learning the English language, which is regarded, not unjustifiably, as the key to the outside world, and obviously this interest will continue to grow. Besides economic interest, the acquisition of English is also educationally important for contemporary China, because English is now the most important carrier of new knowledge. For Chinese learners of most disciplines, the mastery of English is in this regard educationally much more cost-effective than the mastery of any other foreign language. On the intellectual level, the influx of English in China will in the long run greatly benefit the Chinese population, because learning a foreign language enables the learners to realize that things can be described, formulated, or perceived from different angles. With the correct approaches, obtaining a decent grasp of a foreign language can help us develop a more flexible and liberal mind-set, which in turn will even help us to better appreciate our own culture, or be critical about it if necessary. Goethe once said, "Whoever knows no foreign language, knows not even his own."[15] With the increased need for cross-cultural communication, China's further emphasis on English should in the first place be considered in a positive light, as it will indeed bring about positive "capital" for her. Therefore, for any country in the world, including China, tapping into a

globalized language like English is clearly a matter of national interest.

2. *The need of the world to have an international language*: Taking a more cosmopolitan point of view for a globalized world, which is the world we now have, there is unquestionably a high practical value in having a language that is globally understood. It is for this reason that I find expressions like "hegemony" or "imperialism" too emotional, as they very easily prompt us to indulge in historical animosities and distract us from the many positive roles a global language might play. These include, for instance, in areas such as international law and human rights, international rescues and amnesties, academic and scholarly exchanges, urgent medical consultancies, cross-cultural understanding, interreligious dialogues, and so forth. The fact that English rather than French, German, or Esperanto has succeeded in assuming this dominant role should not prevent us from accepting this truth. Even less should it encourage us to take a "boycotting" attitude toward English, which would be against the interests of individual nation-states as well as those of the international community. All in all, despite the critical stance I am going to take, I do not believe that any country, including China, should undermine the importance of a global language like English. The question is only, given the inevitable need to strengthen the use of English, how should individual countries cope with its dominance while preventing its overdominance?

3. *Treating English as an OFL and not as an ENL*: In dealing with language matters, one major rule of thumb is to take linguistic realities seriously. In any human society, the most important linguistic reality is the acquisition of the mother tongue, which is an undeniable fact that should be the starting point of all sensible language policies. While the learning and assimilation of English is culturally and politically inevitable, it remains debatable what attitude or strategy a nation-state should adopt in dealing with English education. A major concern here is that a nation's strategy of English education can only be part of a more generic language strategy, which has to do mainly with policies regarding the native language, so that measures concerning the former must always be discussed with reference to those concerning the latter. It is in this light that we can conceptually differentiate between two strategies of treating English: "optimized foreign language" (OFL) on the one

hand, and "emulated native language" (ENL) on the other. These two English education strategies require some explanation.

By "optimized foreign language," I mean fostering English education as a foreign language with all possible resources and measures while paying full attention to Mother Tongue Literacy (MTL), or the nurturing of the native tongue. Of course, the adoption of an OFL policy is not an easy matter, especially for nations (like China) whose language is typologically dissimilar to English. How under such circumstances can the learning of English be optimized is the task of research on teaching English as a second (foreign) language (TESL/TEFL), which cannot be dealt with in this paper. What we need to emphasize is that, regardless of the extent of the resources a nation might inject into the promotion of English, all this has to be done in parallel with a solid education in the native tongue. If this condition is not met, the whole language strategy will cease to be one of an OFL and degenerate into one of an ENL.

By "emulated native language" (an oxymoron), I mean the strategy of treating English *as if* it were a native language, to the extent that the true native language is severely jeopardized. An ENL is so depicted ("emulated") because it looks away from the linguistic reality of the native tongue and presumptively assumes that, with enough resources, English can be taught and learned as well as if it were a "native language." Of course, given unlimited resources, an ENL is always theoretically possible. But taking into consideration the actual linguistic environment involved and the actual exposure of learners to English, the outcome of an ENL is always limited while its price can be enormously high.[16] And the highest price involved here is not just a matter of money but the alienation of learners from their authentic native tongue, which could have adverse consequences for their intellectual development. Bearing our earlier reference to Leibniz in mind, it is clear that one difference between an OFL and an ENL lies precisely in the different attitudes they embody toward "language care."

The distinction between an OFL and an ENL is meant to single out the former as the more viable and the latter as a self-delusive approach to English education. For a successful implementation of an OFL, various issues have to be carefully considered: besides TESL research as mentioned above, we might need to consider other issues, including the integration of an optimized English curriculum into a basic scheme of mother tongue literacy, the full exploitation of educational technologies, and strategies for the implementation of an OFL in different phases of the educational system.

4. *The medium of instruction of the university curriculum:* For university education in non-English-speaking countries, the holding of conferences, symposia, lectures, and so forth in English as much as possible and the delivery of some courses in English are no doubt beneficial in increasing students' exposure to English. But introducing more English is one thing; changing the language of instruction to English completely or to any extent that might jeopardize the future prospects of the native tongue as an academic language is quite another. We must understand that the university lecture hall is the main platform of the "language care" of any nation-state. It is often the place where the intellectual endeavors of the teacher reach their highest degree of consolidation and creativity. And, most importantly, university teaching is the device through which the culture, scholarship, knowledge, and values of a nation are transmitted from one generation to the other. In a word, as far as "language care" is concerned, university teaching in the mother tongue is a bulwark that no nation can afford to give up without serious cultural and educational consequences.

Besides Germany, one might argue, there are many countries in Europe, such as the Netherlands and the Nordic states, that have started much earlier and gone much further in switching their language of instruction at the university level to English. But we must bear in mind that these countries have much smaller populations than Germany or China, which might have left them with little real choice in the matter.[17] It is well known that the people of these countries tend to speak English extremely well as a second language. Some even argue that for these peoples, English can be considered to be a "second first language" rather than a "first second language." But the general success of these countries in English comes at a high price, for it is obvious that Dutch, Norwegian, or Danish belong to those national languages that have long been overdominated by English, at least in academia.[18] In recent years, there has been a strong tendency for universities in China to adopt more English in their teaching and learning activities, which is largely reasonable. But the crucial question is: How far should we go?

5. *Language care as an unshirkable duty of the entire linguistic community, and of academics in particular*: The German philosopher Herder was of the opinion that if a language is to develop healthfully, it has to be supported by a group of linguistic users (*Publikum*) who are well educated.[19] For any nation-state, university teachers and students are, so to speak, the cream of society. As intellectuals and academics, they all have a duty to learn new knowledge in their respective disciplines as much as possible. But whether the knowledge thus acquired can be successfully retained and transmitted to the school (secondary and primary) and public sectors depends to a large extent on whether these university people can use their native language to recapitulate, reflect on, criticize, apply, and debate the new knowledge gained. It is only through this channel that new knowledge from the outside world can be assimilated and internalized into the mother tongue of the nation, and eventually become a common intellectual asset of the nation and the basis for further conceptual innovation. For academia worldwide, it would probably be a great setback if progress in thought and scholarship could be made only in English!

Therefore, university academics, especially those who have acquired training abroad, should require themselves to publish at least occasionally in their mother tongue (i.e., in addition to English or other languages), despite a possibly smaller and localized readership. Here, I am referring to both the publication of advanced level research papers and to more basic level educational materials such as textbooks. This is the most important way the abstract notion of "language care" can be realized.

6. *The role of language in the natural sciences and in the humanities*: The question regarding how much English and how much native language should be used in academic research has always been a matter of dispute. With regard to this problem, there has been much discussion on the need to treat natural science subjects and humanistic or social scientific subjects differently. One general observation is that the natural sciences deal with universal phenomena that are quite independent of the cultural identity of the researcher, and for that reason, English alone would best serve the purpose of providing a universal medium of communication. On the other hand, it has often been emphasized that for research on humanistic and social scientific subjects, the objects and concepts of

study are in fact not "objective" and "universal" in a natural scientific sense but are significantly motivated by the cultural heritage from which they are derived. Thus, in handling humanistic issues, approaches from different linguistic formulations often provide important contrasts and nuances that lead to a deeper understanding of the issues.[20] It is for this reason that research in the humanities and social sciences should not be confined to or rely on one global language alone. It was along this line of thought that Wolfgang Frühwald, president of the Alexander von Humboldt-Stiftung of Germany, once remarked that

> all cultural and human sciences (in a broader sense all theoretical sciences) have to do with language. Whereas the concept of science in modern natural sciences is a result-oriented one, the concept of science in the human sciences is always process-related. This means that the results of the human sciences are not lying there prior to the process of their description. They are bound to language and style and are therefore not readily [*ohne weiteres*] transferable to one lingua franca.[21]

By the same token, Maurice Godé, a famous French Germanist, once opined that "knowledge of the respective national languages is a basic prerequisite for meaningful study in the humanities."[22]

In short, humanities studies rely on linguistic diversity and on cultural traditions to a much greater extent than do the natural sciences. For the humanities in general and for philosophy in particular, proficiency in one single lingua franca is very often a sign of inadequacy, if not of impoverishment. While this might not apply to Kongzi or Plato, it is certainly true of today's humanities scholar, for whom intercultural understanding and a global outlook have become necessary. As for researchers in the natural sciences, although they do not need a multiplicity of languages to operate, their countries and peoples do need them to fulfill the duty of "language care," which should apply to all disciplines, although to various degrees.

7. *The bargaining power of various native languages in the face of English dominance*: Being *the* language of globalization, it is quite certain that the influence of English will keep growing in the foreseeable future. It seems also inevitable that many languages of the world will succumb to this dominance. The question of how far and how long individual languages can retain their identity and

idiosyncrasies is a matter of cultural dynamics. Generally speaking, a host of factors are involved, of which two are the most crucial: (1) the size of the linguistic community, which proportionally accounts for the multitude of linguistically active authors, and (2) the bulk of the cultural legacy of a language in history, which accounts for the overall attraction for the recurrent use of the language.[23] Taking these factors into consideration, we can give a rough approximation of the future of some languages. Take German as an example: In terms of the size of the linguistic community, there are about 95 million German speakers in Europe, which is considerable compared to other EU languages such as Dutch, Danish, Norwegian, or Swedish. In terms of cultural legacy, contemporary German differs greatly from the German of Leibniz's time because of the richness in literary, philosophical, and other disciplinary classics accumulated over the past two centuries, and this strength, or "capital," might remain significant for many centuries to come. With this bargaining power, will German follow the examples of Dutch or Danish in becoming further marginalized? Or should Germany choose to actively resist such a path?

Take Chinese as another example. Needless to say, the bulk (over 1.3 billion in mainland China alone) and, to a lesser degree, the spread of Chinese speakers in the world are strengths that no one can ignore. As with cultural tradition, the nearly uninterrupted several-thousand-year legacy of Chinese literature, philosophy, art, and so on will obviously render the Chinese language extremely competitive into the distant future. In fact, people often think that while many languages will definitely be conquered or overdominated by English, Chinese is probably among the very few (with Spanish or probably Arabic being two other such candidates) that might eventually be able to truly withstand the onslaught of English, or in the long run even compete with it. But is the future of Chinese really so assured, despite the great bargaining power it possesses?

While such wild guesses might have some point, they might not represent the complete picture. One most important thing we need to bear in mind is that, in addition to the two main factors mentioned above, there are other factors (see note 23) that might complicate the picture, and among these factors we should never leave out two subjective but equally crucial factors: the perseverance of the government in maintaining consistent and favorable language planning policies, and the readiness of members of the linguistic community to contribute to "language care."

8. *What should we aim at when talking about the future of a language? Defending a native language as "object language" or as "operative language":* In our discussion on the likelihood of a nation defending its language in an "englishized" globe, we left out a very important aspect of the issue, namely that a native language can be defended merely as an "object language," or also as an "operative language." By "object language," I mean the language in which intellectual objects such as poetry, philosophy, and history are recorded. By "operative language," I am referring to the language in which we operate when dealing with whatever issues require our attention. Obviously, classical Greek, Latin, or Sanskrit were great languages, but they are nowadays only objects of study because, except for very few users, people no longer operate in them. A pure object language, thanks to the "jewels" it carries, might be safe from immediate extinction, but as long as it does not operate, it is not vital and will never grow. In this regard, Wilhelm von Humboldt was perfectly correct when he said "language is one of the fields whence the general mental power of man emerges in constantly active operation."[24]

Of course, when we talk about using a language to "operate," we might understand operation loosely to embrace everyday usage. But if it is the future academic status of a language that we care about, then we should know that a language might remain in use by a sizable population but lose its esteem as an academic language that is intellectually operable. So we have to know what we are defending!

All of these reckonings are important insofar as they have much to do with the language policies of universities in Germany and elsewhere, including China and Hong Kong. Let me explain this, taking German again as an example. Up to the present moment, German is obviously still both an object language and an operative language, because Kant, Schiller, Weber, or Simmel are still being discussed in German by scholars in Germany and elsewhere. But in case the Germans themselves were to decide to stop using German to lecture or to publish, what would happen, say, in fifty years, or even ten? The truth is very simple: if an academic language stops operating vigorously, it will degenerate quickly into a mere academic object. And this was exactly the warning carried in the open letter to the German politicians.

9. *Language as not merely a tool of expression but as the key to intellectual development; relevance of the mother tongue*: Advocates of English-only policies often adopt a very biased conception of language, which can be called an instrumental view, or the view that language is nothing more than an instrument for expression of what a person already clearly has in mind. But a closer look at the development of modern general linguistics will show that, contrary to this "instrumental" view, linguists are increasingly adopting a "*Bildung*-conception" of language, or the view that language is not merely an instrument for the expression of clear, ready-made ideas but a formative medium through which human intelligence and consciousness can take shape and gradually develop. In other words, for many modern linguists, including Humboldt, Saussure, and Jakobson, language competence and intellectual capacity are equiprimordial and inseparable. If language indeed has such an important role in the development of human intelligence, then the part played by the mother tongue should also be accorded special importance, because the mother tongue is precisely *the* language medium through which all human individuals actually acquire their basic intelligence. Since the acquisition of the mother tongue is a process that is irreversible and inevitable, fostering the learning of English at the cost of the mother tongue (as in the case of an ENL) is like building an edifice on a sand dune or developing a view from nowhere, which is pedagogically problematic and intellectually against the best interests of the learner. This explains why the overdominance of English is such an important problem. It is along this line of thought that some neo-Humboldtian researchers on language have studied the role of the mother tongue, which they think is the very basis for human intellectual existence as well as the very link to our social life-world and to our cultural heritage.[25]

10. *Multilingualism*: Having underlined the importance of the mother tongue for the cultivation and development of human intelligence, it is also important for us to limit this emphasis to prevent this position from degenerating into provincialism or ethnocentrism. In fact, we should note that all of the philosophical justifications that support the primary importance of the mother tongue also lend support to the advantage of supplementing mother tongue learning with the learning of foreign languages. As we suggested at the outset, the learning of a foreign language is

beneficial since it helps to broaden the linguistic-intellectual horizons of learners by providing contrasts in perspectives, formulation strategies, conceptual networks, and so forth. In general linguistics and in philosophy of language, many major theoretical positions are in fact closely related to this issue; for instance, the concept of linguistic value, lexical field theory (*Wortfeldtheorie*), world-picture (*Weltansicht*), the fusion of horizons (*Horizontverschmelzung*), etc. All of these add up to the suggestion that as far as education is concerned, the more languages one learns, the better. Emperor Charles V's dictum, "How many languages one speaks, so many times is he a man,"[26] is a most radical formulation of this position. Naturally, with limited time and resources, there are limits to what can be achieved in the area of multilingualism in education. In order to strike a balance, therefore, I would suggest that, while bilingualism should be a minimum for preuniversity education, education from the undergraduate program onward should at least aim at trilingualism, which should even be made a requirement at the graduate level. Just one word on the concept of "trilingualism": instead of being a mere numerical compromise, many linguistic and philosophical studies have pointed out that the learning of at least three languages exhibits the intellectual advantage of "triangulation"—that is, the prevention of premature antagonism or bipolarity in conceptual comparisons, enabling the learner to thus be more receptive to complexities of our world and better prepared for multilateral discourses.[27]

11. *Toward a glocal language policy in the age of globalization*: Having underlined the importance of English as a global language but warned of its overdominance in local language policies, one general position we arrive at is the adoption of a language policy that is "glocal" in nature. What is a glocal language policy? In short, it is a language policy that is locally rooted but globally perspectivized. In practical terms, it is the combination of MTL and OFL strategies. While the significance of MTL is programmatically self-explanatory and pedagogically fundamental, we must note that an OFL strategy should not be confined to mere TESL or English learning but should include the teaching and learning of any foreign language relevant to one's respective disciplines. With the dominance of English, it is understandable that English will remain globally the most popular foreign language, but this dominance of English should not lead to

monopolization in the world linguistic arena, especially not in academia. Given available resources, foreign languages other than English should never be excluded, for they can and do make contributions of their own to global civilization. In other words, they are valuable cultural "capital" awaiting fruitful investment from every global citizen. If this glocal language policy is adopted consistently by a considerable number of nations with the support of their major universities, then every individual language will have a better future, both locally and internationally. How popular individual languages can become depends naturally on their "bargaining power." So why shouldn't Chinese scholars, depending on their disciplinary needs, learn alongside English some Sanskrit, Greek, Latin, German, French, Tibetan, Japanese, or even Tokharian in order to get the most intellectual benefit? Alternatively, Chinese is obviously a good candidate for all other peoples in the world.[28] Wilhelm von Humboldt once underlined the idiosyncrasies of the Chinese language with the wonderful remarks that Chinese and Sanskrit, despite their antipodal structures, represent the two "fixed extremes" or "end points" of linguistic perfection,[29] and that the Chinese script has "in a certain manner embraced philosophical work within itself."[30]

Educationally speaking, as long as one learns a foreign language seriously enough, whether English or another language, one will be able to get a great deal from the effort. But whatever the combinations, the most important thing is that in any glocal language program the native tongue should always be in place, for without a solid educational foundation in one's native tongue, which is the fountainhead of human intelligence and thus the "true" key to the outside world, all other linguistic maneuvers will become pointless and ineffective. For any country, any attempt to achieve a "better" standard in a foreign language (say, English) at the expense of the native tongue is intellectually and pedagogically unwise and culturally and politically suicidal.

Conclusion

The dominance of English is the result of a long historical process that can hardly be reversed. It is a basic fact that no nation and no government can ignore. Unless a nation does not want to connect economically, politically, intellectually, and culturally with the world, strengthening the use of English is unavoidable. Yet, coming to terms with the dominance of English as an international language is one thing; tolerating its overdominance or allowing English to intrude into domestic language matters is quite another. As I have explained, the overdominance of English amounts to the encroachment and endangerment of other native tongues, but whether or not this scenario should be allowed to prevail is to a large extent in the hands of members of individual linguistic communities, whether government policy makers, university administrators, professors, students, or the general public. What we are dealing with here is our very linguistic human rights, which we might all too easily forsake, if the overdominance of English is accepted without reflection. In this regard, Leibniz's notions of "language care" and of the establishment of a "[mother-tongue]-minded society" are obviously of great heuristic value.

Notes

1. David Crystal, *English as a Global Language*, 2nd ed. (Cambridge: Cambridge University Press, 2003).

2. Robert Philipson and Tove Skutnabb-Kangas, "Englishisation: One Dimension of Globalisation," in David Graddol and Ulrike H. Meinhof, eds., *English in a Changing World* (London: AILA, 1999), pp. 19–36.

3. Pierre Bourdieu, *Language and Symbolic Power*, trans. Gino Raymond and Matthew Adamson (Cambridge: Polity Press, 1991), p. 61; see also Pierre Bourdieu, "The Forms of Capital," in J. Richardson, ed., *Handbook of Theory and Research for the Sociology of Education* (New York: Greenwood Press, 1986), pp. 241–258.

4. See relevant charts in Minoru Tsunoda, "Les Langues internationales dans les publications scientifiques et techniques," *Sophia Linguistica* 13 (1983): 144–155, quoted in Ulrich Ammon, *Ist Deutsch noch internationale Wissenschaftssprache?* (Berlin: Mouton de Gruyter, 1998), pp. 343–362, especially pp. 344, 346.

5. I am borrowing this expression from Richard J. Alexander, "G.lobal L.anguages O.ppress B.ut A.re L.iberating, Too: The Dialectics of English," in Christian Mair, ed., *The Politics of English as a World Language: New Horizons in Postcolonial Cultural Studies* (Amsterdam: Rodopi, 2003), p. 91.

6. Peter von Polenz, *Geschichte der deutschen Sprache* (Berlin: Mouton de Gruyter, 1977), p. 108.

7. The two essays are now available in G. W. F. Leibniz, *Unvorgreifliche Gedanken, betreffend die Ausübung und Verbesserung der deutschen Sprache* (zwei Aufsätze), ed. Uwe Pörksen (Stuttgart: Reclam, 1983).

8. The expression *deutschgesinnt* has to be understood with great care, because before and after Leibniz it has been used with a strong nationalistic flavor, which was not in line with Leibniz's largely cosmopolitan standpoint.

9. This Latin expression can be traced to a letter Leibniz wrote to his friend Gerhard Meier, in which he referred to his German essay "Unvorgreifliche Gedanken …" as "dissertationunculam meam extemporaneam de linguae Germ. Cura" (*Unvorgreifliche Gedanken*, p. 79).

10. Ibid., p. 10.

11. For a fuller account of this prehistory of the German language, see Kwan Tze-wan, "Leibniz and the Development of Modern German: On *Sprachpflege* and the Fate of National Languages" (in Chinese), *Journal of Tongji University* 16, no. 1 (2005): 1–11.

12. On this issue, see George Steiner, "The Hollow Miracle," in George Steiner, ed., *Language and Silence: Essays on Language, Literature, and the Inhuman* (New York: Atheneum, 1967), pp. 101–109.

13. The open letter was initiated by Professors Dieter, Simonis, and Vilmar and was countersigned by thirty-four other professionals from various disciplines (including the humanities, natural sciences, social sciences, and technology). The letter was published on July 24, 2001, and triggered a series of discussions. Related papers are available at http://bibliothek.wz-berlin.de/pdf/2001/p01-003.pdf (accessed May 26, 2005).

14. The same scenario holds, for example, for Denmark, one of the most "englishized" countries in Europe. Philipson and Skutnabb-Kangas reported that the editor in chief of a major Danish national encyclopedia has written that some contributors who are natural scientists are unable to communicate their scholarship in Danish for a Danish audience ("Englishisation," p. 28).

15. "Wer fremde Sprachen nicht kennt, weiss nichts von seiner eigenen" (Johann Wolfgang von Goethe, *Maximen und Reflexionen*, in *Werke* [Berliner Ausgabe] [Berlin: Aufbau, 1960], vol. 18, p. 492). Refer also to a similar dictum usually ascribed to Rudyard Kipling: "What do they know of England who only England know?"

16. Because of previous colonial influence, the English teaching policy in Hong Kong has been exhibiting strong ENL tendencies for decades, with the great abundance of so-called English secondary schools being the most characteristic outcome. With a Chinese population of more than 95 percent, the linguistic ecology for running ENL in Hong Kong is of course not a very favorable one.

17. The populations of Denmark, Norway, Sweden, and the Netherlands in

2005 were 5.43 million, 4.62 million, 9.04 million, and 16.30 million, respectively, compared with Germany's 82.69 million and China's 1.32 billion. See United Nations, "World Population Prospects: The 2004 Revision Population Database," available at http://esa.un.org/unpp/ p2k0data.asp.

18. In 1999, Philipson and Skutnabb-Kangas reported on the situation in Denmark, relying on questionnaires returned by eighty-three academics ("Englishisation," pp. 25–29).

19. Johann Gottfried Herder, *Briefe zu Beförderung der Humanität*, Fünfte Sammlung, §57, *Herders Werke* (Berlin: Aufbau-Verlag, 1982), vol. 5, pp. 108–144, especially pp. 112f., 134f.

20. Regarding the objectivity and universality of objects and concepts in the humanities, see the incisive reflections in Ernst Cassirer, *Zur Logik der Kulturwissenschaften*, 2nd ed. (Darmstadt: Wissenschaftliche Buchgesellschaft, 1961), especially chaps. 1 and 3.

21. Wolfgang Frühwald, "Sprachen öffnen die Welt: Zur Funktion der Nationalsprachen als Sprachen der Wissenschaft" (lecture, Budapest, Beijing, and elsewhere, 2001, available at http://www.humboldt.hu/ HN19/fruhwald.htm [accessed May 24, 2005]). I am indebted to Professor Feng Jun, vice president of Renmin University of China, for bringing Frühwald's lecture to my attention. The English text is my translation of the German text.

22. See a report on Godé's speech at the Universitätstage Heidelberg-Montpellier on January 14, 2004, available at http://www.innovations-report.de/html/berichte/bildung_wissenschaft/bericht-24766.html (accessed May 14, 2005).

23. Besides these two, other important factors determining a language's potential to withstand the overdominance of English include the prestige of a language in the eyes of other nations; the degree of self-esteem of native speakers for the language; the amount of new knowledge carried by a language; the average level of literacy of the respective linguistic community; the abundance of educational materials in the respective language; etc. But these factors will not be discussed in this paper. For some stimulating thoughts on related issues, see Elmar Holenstein, "Ist die viersprachige Schweiz ein Modell für plurikulturelle Staaten?" in Elmar Holenstein, ed., *Kulturphilosophische Perspektiven* (Frankfurt: Suhrkamp, 1998), pp. 11–43. Recently, Holenstein has been actively involved in discussions with me on various linguistic-educational issues, either through e-mail or, during my visit to Yokohama in the summer of 2005, in person.

24. Wilhelm von Humboldt, *Über die Verschiedenheit des menschlichen Sprachbaues und ihren Einfluss auf die geistige Entwicklung des Menschengeschlechts*. Widely known as *Kawi-Schrift* and published in 1835, it is included in *Werke in fünf*

Bänden, vol. 3, *Schriften zur Sprachphilosophie*, ed. Andreas Flitner and Klaus Giel (Stuttgart: Cotta, 1963), p. 391; see also Wilhelm von Humboldt, *On Language: The Diversity of Human Language-Structure and Its Influence on the Mental Development of Mankind*, trans. Peter Heath (Cambridge: Cambridge University Press, 1988), p. 27. Elsewhere, Humboldt made the related statement, "The intellectual merits of language therefore rest exclusively upon the well-ordered, firm and clear mental organization of peoples in the epoch of making or remaking language" (*Kawi-Schrift*, p. 464; *On Language*, p. 81).

25. Among many neo-Humboldtians, Leo Weisgerber proposed in the 1950s the so-called humanistic law of language (*Menschheitsgesetz der Sprache*), which comprises the following three constituent laws: the law of linguistically conditioned human existence, the law of linguistic community, and the law of the mother tongue (*Das Menschheitsgesetz der Sprache als Grundlage der Sprachwissenschaft*, rev. ed. [Heidelberg: Quelle & Meyer, 1964]). Although Weisgerber's theory long ago sank into oblivion because of his overconcentration on German when citing linguistic examples, it seems that the theoretical profile and the basic insights of his work are still highly relevant to our concern today with the overdominance of English and the need to consciously nurture one's mother tongue.

26. Quoted from Arthur Schopenhauer, *Parerga und Paralipomena 2*, zweiter Teilband, *Zürcher Ausgabe, Werke in zehn Bänden* (1859; Zürich: Diogenes, 1977), vol. 10, p. 616: "So viele Sprachen Einer kennt, so viele Mal ist er ein Mensch."

27. For the linguistic and philosophical justification of trilingualism, see *inter alia* the following three texts: (1) Elmar Holenstein, "Ein Dutzend Daumenregeln zur Vermeidung interkultureller Missverständnisse," in Holenstein, ed., *Kulturphilosophische Perspektiven*, pp. 288–312 (English translation: "A Dozen Rules of Thumb for Avoiding Intercultural Misunderstandings," *Polylog*, November 2, 2004, available at http://them. polylog.org/4/ahe-en.htm); (2) Joseph Harold Greenberg, *On Language: Selected Writings of Joseph H. Greenberg*, ed. Keith Denning and Suzanne Kemmer (Stanford, Calif.: Stanford University Press, 1990), especially the chapters on typology and language universals; and (3) Wm. Theodore de Bary, "Asian Classics and Global Education" (lecture delivered on the occasion of the Tang Chun-I Visiting Professorship organized under the auspices of the Philosophy Department of The Chinese University of Hong Kong, January 2005). In this paper, de Bary made the following statement: "At least two other general principles seem applicable to this educational pattern or approach. One is that it is best, if at all possible, for the process to extend to more than one culture other than one's own, so that there is always some point of triangulation and a multicultural

perspective predominates over simplistic we/they, self/other, East/West comparisons."

28. Owing to the growing popularity of Chinese, an examination scheme for Chinese proficiency known as HSK (Hanyu Shuiping Kaoshi, nicknamed the Chinese TOEFL) is now in operation in thirty-three countries (and more than eighty cities) around the world. For related information, see the HSK main site, http://www.hsk.org.cn/, or http://www.hsk.org.cn/test_arrangement/gw.asp for the complete list of international examination points.

29. Humboldt, *Kawi-Schrift*, p. 676; *On Language*, p. 232. For further discussion, see Kwan Tze-wan, "Wilhelm von Humboldt on the Chinese Language," *Journal of Chinese Linguistics* 29, no. 2 (2001): 169–242.

30. Wilhelm von Humboldt, *Lettre à Abel-Rémusat sur la nature des formes grammaticales en général et sur le génie de la langue chinoise en particulier* (Paris: Librairie Orientale de Dondey-Dupré, 1827).

Bibliography

Alexander, Richard J. "G.lobal L.anguages O.ppress B.ut A.re L.iberating, Too: The Dialectics of English." In Christian Mair, ed., *The Politics of English as a World Language: New Horizons in Postcolonial Cultural Studies*. Amsterdam: Rodopi, 2003.

Ammon, Ulrich, ed. *The Dominance of English as a Language of Science: Effects on Other Languages and Language Communities*. Berlin: Mouton de Gruyter, 2001.

———. *Ist Deutsch noch internationale Wissenschaftssprache?* Berlin: Mouton de Gruyter, 1998.

Apel, Karl-Otto. "Noam Chomsky's Theory of Language and Contemporary Philosophy: A Case Study in the Philosophy of Science." In *Towards a Transformation of Philosophy*. Translated by Glyn Adey and David Fisby. London: Routledge, 1980.

Bourdieu, Pierre. "The Forms of Capital." In J. Richardson, ed., *Handbook of Theory and Research for the Sociology of Education*. New York: Greenwood Press, 1986.

——— *Language and Symbolic Power*. Translated by Gino Raymond and Matthew Adamson. Cambridge: Polity Press, 1991.

Calvet, Louis-Jean. *Language Wars*. Translated by Michel Petheram. Oxford: Oxford University Press, 1998.

Cassirer, Ernst. *Zur Logik der Kulturwissenschaften*. 2nd ed. Darmstadt: Wissenschaftliche Buchgesellschaft, 1961.

Coulmas, Florian, ed. *A Language Policy for the European Community: Prospect and Quandaries*. Berlin: Mouton de Gruyter, 1991.

Crystal, David. *English as a Global Language.* 2nd ed. Cambridge: Cambridge University Press, 2003.

de Bary, Wm. Theodore. "Asian Classics and Global Education." Lecture delivered on the occasion of the Tang Chun-I Visiting Professorship organized under the auspices of the Philosophy Department of The Chinese University of Hong Kong, January 2005.

Eucken, Rudolf. *Geschichte der philosophischen Terminologie im Umriss.* 1879. Reprint, Hildesheim: Olms, 1964.

Graddol, David, and Ulrike H. Meinhof, eds. *English in a Changing World.* London: AILA, 1999.

Greenberg, Joseph Harold. *Language, Culture, and Communication.* Stanford, Calif.: Stanford University Press, 1971.

———. *On Language: Selected Writings of Joseph H. Greenberg.* Edited by Keith Denning and Suzanne Kemmer. Stanford, Calif.: Stanford University Press, 1990.

Herder, Johann Gottfried. *Briefe zu Beförderung der Humanität.* Fünfte Sammlung, §57, *Herders Werke,* vol. 5, pp. 108–144, especially pp. 112f., 134f. Berlin: Aufbau-Verlag, 1982.

Holenstein, Elmar, ed. *Kulturphilosophische Perspektiven.* Frankfurt: Suhrkamp, 1998.

Humboldt, Wilhelm von. *On Language: The Diversity of Human Language-Structure and Its Influence on the Mental Development of Mankind.* Translated by Peter Heath. Introduction by Hans Aarsleff. Cambridge: Cambridge University Press, 1988.

Kwan Tze-wan. "Leibniz and the Development of Modern German: On *Sprachpflege* and the Fate of National Languages" (in Chinese). *Journal of Tongji University* 16, no. 1 (2005): 1–11.

———. "Wilhelm von Humboldt on the Chinese Language." *Journal of Chinese Linguistics* 29, no. 2 (2001): 169–242.

Leibniz, G. W. F. *Unvorgreifliche Gedanken, betreffend die Ausübung und Verbesserung der deutschen Sprache* (zwei Aufsätze). Edited by Uwe Pörksen. Stuttgart: Reclam, 1983.

Mair, Christian, ed. *The Politics of English as a World Language: New Horizons in Postcolonial Cultural Studies.* Amsterdam: Rodopi, 2003.

Ostler, Nicholas. *Empires of the Word: A Language History of the World.* London: HarperCollins, 2005.

Philipson, Robert. *English Imperialism.* Oxford: Oxford University Press, 1992.

Polenz, Peter von. *Geschichte der deutschen Sprache.* Berlin: Mouton de Gruyter, 1977.

Saussure, Ferdinand de. *Course in General Linguistics.* Edited by Charles Bally and Albert Sechehaye, in collaboration with Albert Riedlinger. Translated, with an introduction and notes, by Wade Baskin. New York: McGraw-Hill, 1972.

Schierholz, Stefan J., ed. *Die deutsche Sprache in der Gegenwart: Festschrift für Dieter Cherubim zum 60. Geburtstag.* Frankfurt am Main: Peter Lang, 2001.

Scholten, Dirk. *Sprachverbreitungspolitik des nationalsozialistischen Deutschlands.* Frankfurt am Main: Peter Lang, 2000.

Schopenhauer, Arthur. *Parerga und Paralipomena 2. Zweiter Teilband, Zürcher Ausgabe. Werke in zehn Bänden,* vol. 10. 1859. Reprint, Zürich: Diogenes, 1977.

Skutnabb-Kangas, Tove, and Robert Philipson, eds. *Linguistic Human Rights: Overcoming Linguistic Discrimination.* Berlin: Mouton de Gruyter, 1994.

Steiner, George. *Language and Silence: Essays on Language, Literature, and the Inhuman.* New York: Atheneum, 1967.

Weisgerber, Leo. *Das Menschheitsgesetz der Sprache als Grundlage der Sprachwissenschaft.* Rev. ed. Heidelberg: Quelle & Meyer, 1964.

Witt, Jörg. *Wohin steuern die Sprachen Europas?* Tübingen: Stauffenburg, 2001.

Wolff, Gerhard, ed. *Deutsche Sprachgeschichte.* Stuttgart: Reclam, 1984.

Appendix 1

Life Chronology of Tang Junyi

Lau Kwok-keung

1909   Born January 17 in Yibin, Sichuan province, China. Father was a scholar of less than modest means. The eldest son, Tang had one brother and four sisters, one of whom died young.

1911   Started study of Chinese characters with his mother when he was two years old.

1919   Entered the primary school of the First Normal University of Sichuan Province in Chengdu, Sichuan.

1921   Entered Chongqing United Secondary School in Chongqing, Sichuan province.

1925   Graduated from Chongqing United Secondary School. Went to Beijing to continue studies at the Sino-Russian University. After one term, transferred to the Philosophy Department of Beijing University, where he stayed for one year. Then transferred to the Philosophy Department of Southeast University in Nanjing (later renamed Central University).

1931   Father died leaving family without the resources even for his own burial, which was not accomplished until three months later.

LAU Kowk-keung is associate professor in the Department of Philosophy, The Chinese University of Hong Kong.

1932   Graduated from Central University, Nanjing, but remained in the Philosophy Department as a teaching assistant. Supported whole family with his limited remuneration.

1937   July 7, Japanese troops invaded Shanghai and Nanjing. Tang returned to Chengdu and taught in the Chinese Western University as well as in some secondary schools there.

1940   Met Mou Tsung-san, renowned contemporary Confucian scholar, who became his lasting friend.

1943   Returned to Chongqing and married Tse Ting Kwong, a graduate in educational psychology.

1946   Central University moved from Chongqing back to Nanjing. Continued to teach in the Philosophy Department of Central University until he moved with Mou Tsung-san to Wusi, where they taught in Southern Yangzi University in Jiangsu.

1949   As the military situation worsened, he, together with Qian Mu, went to Canton to teach at the private Wa Kiu University. Two months later they moved to Hong Kong.

1949   October, Tang and Qian started a postsecondary college, the Asia Evening College of Arts and Commerce.

1950   March, with the financial assistance of a businessman, the Evening College was restructured to become New Asia College, which later, in 1963, became a founding college of The Chinese University of Hong Kong. At New Asia College served as registrar of the college as well as head of the Department of Philosophy and Education. Arranged 139 cultural lectures open to the public every Saturday in the period 1951 to 1954. He himself was one of the chief speakers.

1956   August, made his first visit to Taiwan.

1957   Invited by the U.S. government to make a tour of the United States, where he met such scholars as William E. Hocking, Brand Blanshard, Sidney Hook, D. T. Suzuki, Herrlee Creel, Wing-tsit Chan, et al. Also visited Japan and Europe in his round-the-world trip.

1958   Joined with Chang Chun-mai, Mou Tsung-san, Hsu Fu-kuan to publish *Chinese Culture and the World: Our Common Understanding of Chinese Academic Research and the Future of Chinese Culture and World Culture* as a manifesto affirming the values of Chinese culture.

1962 Founded the Eastern Humanity Association and was elected its chairman.

1963 The Chinese University of Hong Kong was founded, and he became the first chair professor of the Philosophy Department, as well as chairman of the Philosophy Board of Studies and dean of the Faculty of Arts.

1966 March, due to the detachment of the retina of his left eye, went to America for treatment, which proved unsuccessful. In December, went to Kyoto, Japan, for treatment and stayed for eight months, enjoying its cultural ambience.

1972 Participated in a conference held in Hawaii on the 500th anniversary of Wang Yangming.

1973 Retired from The Chinese University of Hong Kong.

1974 Together with eight other governors of New Asia College, resigned to protest the merging of the three colleges of The Chinese University of Hong Kong in violation of the earlier guarantee of their autonomy.

1975 Invited by Taiwan University as visiting professor for eight months.

1976 August 12, diagnosed as having lung cancer.

1978 February 2, died of lung cancer in Baptist Hospital, Hong Kong.

Notes on the Principal Publications of Tang Junyi

Professor Tang published his first article in 1926, "On Hsuen Tze's [Xunzi] Theory of Human Nature." In 1929, he wrote his first paper still extant, "A New Interpretation of Mencius' Theory of Nature."

In the 1940s, his publications concerned mainly the sentiments of life and moral self-reflection, such as *The Sympathy of Life* (1944) and *The Establishment of the Moral Self* (1944).

A second phase came in the 1950s, with his reflections on

Chinese culture, such as *The Spiritual Values of Chinese Culture* (1953), *The Re-establishment of Humanistic Spirit* (1955), *Cultural Consciousness and Moral Reason*, vols. 1, 2 (1958), and *The Development of Chinese Humanistic Spirit* (1958).

A third phase came in the 1960s and 1970s, in which he published six volumes of reflections in a series on the sources of Chinese philosophy, such as *On the Sources of Chinese Philosophy: Introduction* (1966), *On the Sources of Chinese Philosophy: Human Nature* (1968), and *On the Sources of Chinese Philosophy: Tao* (1973).

Two volumes entitled *Life Existence and the Horizons of Mind* (1977) constituted the fourth and final phase of his publications and the completion of his system of philosophy.

Appendix 2

⤝⧆⤞

The Chinese at Columbia: A Personal Testament

When I was first asked by Professor Bernadette Li to speak at this luncheon on "Columbia and China,"[1] I thought she wanted me to talk about prominent Chinese in the life of Columbia, something on the order of what I wrote for the Living Legacies series in *Columbia Magazine* about "Columbia's Early Start in East Asian Studies." But Professor Li quickly disabused me of this idea. No, she said, we want you to talk about your own experience at Columbia.

That is, of course, a somewhat different matter, because it means approaching the topic from the Columbia side, instead of starting with the Chinese (i.e., with the story of Dean Lung, who took the initiative to set up Chinese studies here at the turn of the twentieth century), and instead starting from where I was in 1937, as a freshman at Columbia, when I took my first steps in Chinese studies, brought to this point very much as an outgrowth of Columbia's own internal evolution as an educational institution.

By now some of you are no doubt aware that the special signature of Columbia's undergraduate program is the Core Curriculum, consisting initially of the Contemporary Civilization course, to which was added the Literature Humanities course in 1937. At the first meeting of the Contemporary Civilization course in my freshman year, Professor (later Dean) Carman said, "Of course you understand that this course does not include all of world civilization. This is only contemporary civilization in the West. We need to add Asian civilizations to the program, and I hope some of you will think of how you might prepare yourselves so as to include Asia in a more global view of civilization." At that time, as a mere freshman, I had no clear idea of what I wanted to do, but I decided to start Chinese the next year, and I could do so because Columbia was one of a very few universities that offered Chinese in the 1930s.

This adventure into Chinese studies was very much a reflection of Columbia's own unique institutional development—something one would not have been led to at a college that lacked a core curriculum focusing on the issues of what constitutes a civilization, and therefore how China qualifies as a civilization rather than as an object of exotic interest on the part of the cultural dilettante. Certainly in the America of the 1930s there was already that exotic interest, and there was also the contemporary interest in China as the scene of revolutionary changes mainly instigated from the West. But the idea of trying to understand China as a mature civilization embodying its own values, and not as a stagnant or retrograde society, ripe for revolutionary change and radical restructuring, was rare at that time.

When I started Chinese in 1938, the class was small, and included an odd assortment of missionary types (the teacher himself, Carrington Goodrich, was of missionary stock) and, by contrast, leftists attracted to revolutionary China, of which I was one at that moment, and the black singer Paul Robeson, who had become enamored of Mao and his revolution. Another odd character was a German woman who later turned out to be a Nazi spy using academic study as a cover for her undercover work.

As a young socialist in my teens I too had something of a romantic interest in Mao, but I was disabused of this by the wake-up call of the pact in 1939 between Stalin and Hitler, which left Hitler free to attack Western Europe and the Jews, and then Mao's subsequent following of Stalin and the Comintern line, unacceptable to me as a democratic socialist. From this point on I became increasingly skeptical of the dominant Marxist and pseudo-Marxist interpretations of Chinese history and society, and I became determined to establish an interpretive base within Chinese tradition itself, as free as possible of all Eurocentric theories and ideologies. In other words I would undertake the kind of study of China and Asian civilization that was already integral to the core course in Contemporary Civilization itself—as a self-conscious reexamination of the values underlying Western civilization, and I found that indeed there was the same kind of self-conscious reexamination and critique of Chinese civilization within the tradition itself.

Before I had gone very far with this, my studies were interrupted—or should I say diverted—by World War II, my involvement in the study of Japanese, and my service in naval intelligence in the Pacific theater. But what then appeared to be a digression from my original course proved in fact to be a gain, because as I continued, after the war, to pursue Japanese studies alongside of Chinese, I became aware of the importance of Japanese civilization as a reflection *on* (not of, but on) Chinese civilization. As a matter of fact, during the Pacific War I also, unexpectedly, became exposed to Koreans (forced laborers under the Japanese in the Pacific) and the Ryukyuans, encountered on the Okinawan campaign. All of these peoples, historically much influenced by the Chinese, had their own take on Chinese civilization—their own angle of approach to it, their own interpretation. In other words, they were seasoned, experienced interpreters of Chinese civilization, and I as a neophyte could benefit from seeing what they found of importance, of value, in Chinese civilization. When then I was able to resume my Chinese studies after the war, I had multiple perspectives from which to view China as a mature civilization, central to all East Asia, and not just as the subject—or indeed victim—of Eurocentric ideologies.

This process was already begun in my postwar graduate studies at Columbia, but those studies were handicapped by the lack of any scholars here with an in-depth knowledge of Chinese philosophy and intellectual history. If I wanted to see China from within I had to go to China itself to complete my graduate studies. And now, against this background, I was looking for scholars who could speak to the core issues of Chinese civilization, as the Chinese themselves defined them, in the same way as Western thinkers defined the issues for Western civilization.

When I went to Beijing in 1948 to continue my studies, I was extremely fortunate in having the help and advice of two distinguished Chinese scholars who had studied at Columbia under John Dewey, Hu Shih and Fung Yu-lan. Dr. Hu at that time was president of Beijing National University, but his scholarly work was in Chinese philosophy and history and touched on many areas I had become involved in. The same was true of Fung Yu-lan, then teaching Chinese philosophy at Tsinghua University. But neither of them was particularly conversant with the seventeenth-century political thought of Huang Zongxi, whom I was studying, or with Huang's *Mingyi daifang lu* (later translated by me as *Waiting for the Dawn*), a major critique of Chinese dynastic rule from a Confucian/Mencian point of view. It turned out in fact that my best Chinese mentor was Huang himself. As I tried to understand his critique of a wide range of Chinese political, economic, and social problems, I was compelled to explore the major institutional histories of China by such eminent Song and Ming scholars as Zheng Qiao, Ma Duanlin, Wang Yinglin, Qiu Jun, and many others. And as I tried to understand the intellectual context of Huang's work, by studying his monumental histories of Song and Ming Confucian thought, he became my primary teacher in things Chinese.

At the fall of Beijing in late 1948, I was forced to relocate to Lingnan University, where I encountered other refugee scholars, and still others at New Asia College, then being set up in Hong Kong by leading scholars in exile like Qian Mu and Tang Junyi. Qian Mu was a true giant in the later intellectual history of premodern China. Tang was a major figure in the revival of Confucian philosophy. From both of them I learned much that was then terra incognita to Western scholarship, and I consider myself fortunate that I was able later to pay tribute to them through honorary lectureships that I held at The Chinese University of Hong Kong (successor to New Asia College).

The most immediate fruit of my apprenticeship in the study of Chinese history and thought at the hands of these mature Chinese scholars was a series of conferences on Chinese thought that I conducted in the United States under the auspices of the American Council of Learned Societies, to which I invited such scholars, and from which emanated several symposium volumes that opened up a new world to American scholarship. The later fruit of this scholarly association is to be found in my own books dealing with such issues as self and society in Neo-Confucian thought, the philosophy of the mind-and-heart in Neo-Confucianism, what I called the Liberal Tradition in China (dealing with liberal learning and liberal education), and civil society and human rights, etc.

On my return to the United States, however, I found myself responsible for developing a new program of general education in Asian civilization and humanities, in fulfillment of Harry Carman's hope expressed back in 1937. This development occupied me much of the time in the 1950s and 1960s, producing source readings, translations, teaching guides, etc., for use in general education on Asia—by now over one hundred volumes of relevant materials. In addition to service as chair of the East Asian Department, I was diverted from my scholarly work by almost ten years of service to the university during the crisis of the late 1960s and 1970s, some as a leader of the new University Senate and then as provost and chief academic officer, from 1971 to 1978.

I call these "digressions" from my principal Chinese studies, but there are two respects in which these external involvements have shaped the way in which I view China itself. The study and teaching of Asian civilization has led me, as I said earlier, always to view Chinese civilization not only as entitled to respect in itself but also as the center of East Asian civilizations that are not simply reducible to aspects of Sinic civilization. In the case of my own special interest in Confucianism, this manifests itself not only as a Chinese contribution to civilization at large but as a cultural movement extending beyond China that is also multicultural. As such it cannot be seen just as Chinese property. Educationally speaking its future is tied up with the future of East Asian civilization as a whole, and its contribution should be seen as potentially one to global education as a whole.

Recently I was asked by scholars at the National Taiwan University to speak on the crisis of humanities education in an increasingly hi-tech society and educational system. This January I am speaking on the same subject at The Chinese University of Hong Kong in lectures honoring the aforementioned Tang Junyi. It is all well and good for the Confucian Association in Beijing to reverse the anti-Confucian direction of Mao's cultural revolution, and now to affirm Confucianism as the heart of Chinese civilization, but it is another to recognize that Confucian humanism has had a life of its own outside mainland China, and is not to be seen as simply identifiable with one China. Taiwan, Hong Kong, Singapore, Korea, and Japan all have their own parts to play, and I would hope the same would be true of Columbia itself, where Chinese and Confucian studies were kept alive through the Cultural Revolution of the 1960s and 1970s.

The fact that they were kept alive here during the dark days of the Cultural Revolution reminds me of something I wrote at the height of that assault on Chinese tradition (a piece published later in a volume dedicated to the aforementioned Tang Junyi). At that time (1970) I predicted that the Great Proletarian Cultural Revolution would fail to eradicate Confucianism:

> The unfortunate aspect of their modern revolutionary experience has been a temporary loss of their own self-respect and a denial of their right to assimilate new experience by a process of reintegration with the old. The consequences of that alienation and its violent backlash have only been too evident in the Cultural Revolution. We may be sure, however, that the process of growth is only hidden, not stopped, and that the new experience of the Chinese people will eventually be seen in significant part as a growth emerging from within and not simply as a revolution inspired from without.[2]

Confirmation of what I said then came less than ten years later; after the close of the Cultural Revolution, the death of Mao, and the inception of the Deng regime, China opened up again, I was allowed back into China, and renewed my old acquaintance with people like Fung Yu-lan. I invited Fung to revisit Columbia, which he did in 1982, recalling his happy experience on Morningside, "on the banks of the majestic Hudson," as he put it, and working as a library assistant for the Chinese collection in Low Library. Indeed when he gave an address on accepting an honorary degree, he spoke from this very podium in the Rotunda. In his opening remarks, he quoted some famous lines from the *Classic of Odes*: "Zhou is an ancient kingdom and now its charge is renewed." By Zhou he meant China and by its "charge" he meant China's civilizing mission—thus, as I say, confirming my own affirmation, in darker days that he too lived through, of China's enduring Way.

That China has been able to make a contribution to world civilization is attributable to the dedication and enduring qualities of such scholars as these, who survived through most trying times. In this respect I think of Dr. Hu Shih, long after our days in Beijing, who was often my host at the Academia Sinica in Taiwan when I was doing research there. He often had me to lunch, as a break from my long hours in the library there, and shared with me some of his own reading notes on the writings of Huang Zongxi. One memento of him that I treasure comes from the time that he was a refugee from Communism in the United States during the early 1950s. It was a fund-raising appeal in support of other scholars who had taken refuge in the United States, an effort to which he lent his name as a former ambassador to the United States and owing to his importance as a scholar relatively well known in America. On the cover of this appeal is an inscription in Hu Shih's distinctive calligraphy, a quotation from the *Analects.* It has to do with the nature and character of the *shi* or *shih,* a term susceptible of translation into English in many ways because it connotes several different leadership qualities of the noble person: originally something like knight or gentleman, depending on whether you emphasize its military or civil aspects. Hu Shih translated *shi* as "scholar" because he was indeed thinking about modern scholars; the Japanese tended to equate it with samurai, as the ideal of the self-sacrificing dedicated warrior. My own translation of the passage renders it as "he who would serve as a leader," and goes as follows: "He who would serve as a leader must be stouthearted and enduring, for his burden is heavy and his Way is long. [The original text in the *Analects* continues:] To be truly humane is the burden he takes upon himself; is that not heavy? His Way lasts until death—is that not long?"

These days we hear much about the "public intellectual" as a scholar with a social conscience and an active sense of public responsibility. To my mind scholarship is necessarily public, as is teaching, but we recognize that this responsibility attaches to leadership and service in almost any endeavor. Hu Shih himself exemplified such scholarship and leadership. So too did many of the other scholars I have spoken of, early and late, who carried on their work in difficult times against great odds. Regardless of where you might put them today on the political spectrum of left or right, each stood for recognizable human ideals and was willing to suffer hardship and exile for these. If there is anything that typifies what China and Confucianism have to contribute to a global education or to the humanistic learning Columbia is supposed to stand for, I would say, this is it.

Before concluding my recollections of distinguished Chinese Columbians I have known, let me note, with great sadness, the recent demise of my dear friend and classmate Nian-tzu (N. T.) Wang, a noted economist who served China at the United Nations for many years. He and I were indeed more than mere classmates in the class of 1941, Columbia College. Indeed we were floor mates in John Jay

Hall our freshman year, and I still remember him as a slender, friendly young man with a gentility of manner that I learned to appreciate more and more as the mark of a well-bred Chinese.

From that point on we were good, but not the very closest, friends. When I decided to take up Chinese studies that same year, you could not expect us to show up in the same class. N. T. did not come to Columbia to start Chinese, nor, when the war started after our graduation, was he likely to become a Japanese language officer, as I and my friend Donald Keene did.

But I remained aware of his progress in the study of economics and his rise to great eminence in that field, and since he was a loyal alumnus of the class of 1941, we always enjoyed sharing experiences at annual class reunions.

Here let me just recall one of those occasions that was especially memorable for me. In the 1980s I was invited by the Institute of East Asian Philosophies, National University of Singapore, to give a series of public lectures on Confucianism. At the conclusion of the series I was honored at a banquet hall downtown, but as I came into the lobby of the hall, I noticed a great banner stretched across the front of the atrium. It said in bold Chinese characters, "A warm welcome and congratulations to the distinguished visiting scholar, Wang Nian-tzu." Perhaps no one realized when it was left hanging there that it would be seen by the incoming guest the next evening who would happen to be an old friend of N. T.'s.

I should not end this memoir without recalling another episode, unconnected with the matters discussed here but not unrelated to the subject of "Columbia and the Chinese." It is my early acquaintance with Wellington Koo (1908 B.A., 1912 Ph.D.) at the end of World War II. After three years of service in the Pacific and the Occupation of Japan, I was reassigned to Washington in 1946 (having by then reached the rank of lieutenant commander) as head of the Far Eastern desk in the Office of Naval Intelligence. One of my duties was as an official observer of the meetings of the Far Eastern Commission, representing the Allied powers in the setting of overall policy for the Japanese Occupation, and for fixing guidelines for General MacArthur as Supreme Commander of the Allied Powers (SCAP). MacArthur's performance as SCAP drew most of the attention of the media and the historians, but considering the divergent ideologies and power interests among the so-called Allies, there was a considerable potential for political mischief, if not outright conflict, within the commission setting Occupation policy. During the period I observed it, however, Wellington Koo (then Chinese ambassador to the United States) served as chairman of the commission and demonstrated his superb diplomatic skills in achieving policy consensus among the Allies. I was greatly impressed by his deft handling of things. With a lifetime of learning still ahead of me, I knew enough even then to appreciate a real master at work. His quiet success was itself the reason more was not heard of him then.

Notes

1. "Columbia's Chinese Connection" (conference, Columbia University, September 10–11, 2004).
2. Wm. Theodore de Bary, ed., *The Unfolding of Neo-Confucianism* (New York: Columbia University Press, 1975), p. 32.